WATER IN THE WILDERNESS

WATER
IN THE WILDERNESS

Understanding the Bible

T. G. CHIFFLOT

Translated by
Luke O'Neill

HERDER AND HERDER

1967
HERDER AND HERDER NEW YORK
232 Madison Avenue, New York 10016

Original edition: *Comprendre la Bible,*
Paris, Les Editions du Cerf, 1965.

Nihil obstat: Thomas J. Beary, Censor Librorum
Imprimatur: †Robert F. Joyce, Bishop of Burlington
September 19, 1966

Contents

Foreword, by Ignatius Hunt, O.S.B.   7
Introduction   9

FIRST PART:
LIVING WATER AND THE WILDERNESS
Principles for a Reading of the Bible

How is the Bible to be Read?   13
   I. Do We Have to Read the Bible?   15
  II. Living Water and the Wilderness   19
 III. Some Principles for Understanding Scripture   27
     1. The Bible, Word of God and Human Word   28
     2. The Inspiration of Holy Scripture   30
     3. The Meaning and the Meanings of Scripture   38
     4. Scripture and Tradition   45
 IV. Various Ways of Reading the Bible   49

SECOND PART:
THE SWORD AND THE WORD
Simple Thoughts to Nourish Our Faith

   I. The Bible is a Sacred History   55
  II. The Bible is a Promise   58
 III. The Bible is the Book of Christ   62
 IV. The Bible is the Book of the Church   66
  V. The Bible is a Mirror   70
 VI. The Bible is the Book of Prayer   75

THIRD PART:
THE LETTER AND THE SPIRIT
Some Notes for Further Reflection

I. Biblical Questions and the Life of the Church Today   81
   1. Biblical Questions and the Crisis in Culture   82
   2. The Biblical Movement   91
II. Literal and Religious Exegesis of the Old Testament   97
III. The Demands of Translation. The Psalms   107
IV. The Professors and the Imagination   116

CONCLUSION: ENCOUNTER WITH CHRIST
The Source and End of Scripture

Encounter With Christ   133

Index   139

Foreword

The death of Père Thomas G. Chifflot, O.P., in August, 1964, long-time biblical editor of Les Editions du Cerf, was a great loss. Although frail and never in very good health, he was strong in spirit, friendly to all, and an enterpriser in the best sense of the term. He was the moving spirit behind the Jerusalem Bible in its various forms and editions, the *Lectio Divina* series, and many other projects, volumes, and booklets.

During my stay at the Ecole Biblique in Jerusalem, Père Chifflot was there for a week in the spring of 1963 to discuss various long-term publication projects with the Faculty. However, he also consented to give a conference in very informal style to all those who wished to meet with him in the recreation room of the Ecole. Exuding a spirit of warmth and humility, he told us how the Church historian Henri I. Marrou had been invited to give a conference and was shown to a large throne on which was inscribed in large letters the one word VERITAS. When he saw that word he refused to use the throne, stating that while he sought the truth in his historical research he could not measure up to the rigid standards which that throne seemed to impose upon its occupants. Père Chifflot applied this to himself, humbly stating that he was not a scholar at all, but merely helped scholars publish their writings as a form of apostolate. As the afternoon wore on and as he discussed the various projects under consideration at that time (some of which are now completed), most of us realized that if we weren't speaking with a scholar he was about as close to it as one could get without falling into that category; and we certainly knew that we were in the presence of a man of God—a "biblical man" of top quality.

Prior to that acquaintance I had come across several fine essays by Père Chifflot, always written with the idea of making the Bible loved and understood, and the present volume is a prolongation of that same idea. *Water in the Wilderness* is as solid as the rock from which the water flowed, and I have enjoyed reading both the French original and the smoothly flowing English translation. This is a book from which all can learn. It provides an excellent introduction to the Bible for adult beginners and it may well serve as a good rejuvenating agent for those whose love of Scripture needs rekindling.

It is a pleasure to pay homage to one of the great animators of the modern biblical renewal, and I can state without any feeling of exaggeration whatsoever that the person who does not share Père Chifflot's enthusiasm for the Christian life in general and for the inspired Scriptures in particular through reading this book is losing a wonderful opportunity. The book stands as a worthy memorial to its highly respected author and is a distinct credit to the publishing firm of Herder and Herder from whom so many fine books on Sacred Scripture have come to us.

Conception Abbey   *Ignatius Hunt, O.S.B.*
Conception, Missouri

Introduction

THE *purpose of this book is to help the reader hear in the Bible the Word of God. The hurried reader, as he searches for easy formulas, must first be put on his guard, though, for there are no easy formulas.*

Scripture will never reach our understanding as God's word unless we, while reading it or listening to it as it is read, experience a change of heart—unless we possess an attitude of active faith. The simple truth is that the sacred text is God's Word only because of the meaning which God has given to it, and this meaning is only accessible to Faith. This was the reason why the Church Fathers insisted that study alone was insufficient for mastering sacred language. Only the Spirit who inspired it at the time of its utterance can make it understood. Our purpose, then, must constantly be "to rise to the crest of inspiration."

But it would be hardly less disastrous if we separated attentiveness to the Word of God from attentiveness to human language, an attentiveness which calls for precise, demanding study, and for knowledge of language's laws. It was only at the term of a long human relationship with Jesus that the apostles exclaimed, "You are the Christ, the Son of the living God." And, in like fashion, it is only after persevering and frequently arduous struggle with the biblical text that the Bible becomes for the reader "a spring of water welling up to eternal life."

This twofold demand is of the very nature of Scripture, which is both human word and message of God. Just as Christ is God even to His very humanity, so the Word of God is human even to its very divinity. We can no more readily hear the Word of God without first listening to the human word of the inspired writers than we can know God without going the way of the humanity of Christ.

FIRST PART

LIVING WATER
AND THE WILDERNESS

Principles for a Reading of the Bible

How is the Bible to be Read?

Who could pretend to give the answer to a question which so many Christians are asking?

The answer, after all, is given by the Bible itself to everyone who, in docility to the Spirit who inspired it, reads the Bible with the Church which has preserved it. The efforts we make to learn how to read the Bible cannot be a simple matter of mastering a human technique. They must be directed towards increased attentiveness to the *mystery* of the Word of God—a mystery which will always surpass any methods and ways of thinking of ours.

My sole intention here is to try to present an approach to this mystery. In doing this, I willingly join the company of the many Christians today who, upon opening the Bible, discover a path of progress from wonder towards confusion. I would like, if I can, to help them over a good many questions which may have been rather badly phrased. I make no pretense, however, of using any other light for illuminating their difficulties than the light of the Bible itself. If I then risk suggesting, as did Duguet, a few "principles for the understanding of Holy Scripture" and some "different ways of reading the Bible," it should be clearly understood that the "principles" are intended solely to direct attention towards the mystery of the Bible (which cannot be limited by these "principles"), and that the "methods" have value only through docility to the Spirit who must inspire them all.

But there is a preliminary question which must first be answered.

I.

Do We Have to Read
the Bible?

THERE is no point in taking a lot of time over an answer to this question, for the answer is clear. It can be summed up in three propositions: it is not obligatory; it is not prohibited; it is recommended.

(a) *It is not obligatory*. Let it be fully understood that direct, personal reading of the sacred text is not an absolute necessity for salvation. There are many documents in the Church's magisterium[1] which make this clear by condemning propositions such as Quesnel's, for example: "It is useful and necessary, everywhere and for all categories of men, to study and to know first of all the spirit, the piety, and the mysteries of Holy Scripture."[2]

Such condemnations can cause surprise and we must carefully weigh their significance. The popes evidently have no intention of denying that faithful adherence to divine revelation—whose primary source is the Word of God as recorded in the Bible—is absolutely necessary for salvation. What they do deny is that

---

[1] They are to be found in Denzinger, *Enchiridion Symbolorum,* nos. 1429–1435, 1567, 1604–1606, 1607–1608, 1630–1633.

[2] See Denzinger, no. 2667.

each of the faithful must, of necessity, have personal recourse to the biblical text. An affirmation of that sort would betoken a misunderstanding both of the position which the Bible holds in the Church's teaching and of the organic unity of the Church which teaches and the Church which is taught: the ordinary Christian who without reading the Bible listens to the Church, already lives by the Bible. This is why—and there is good reason to repeat it—the "enlightened" Christian who is familiar with the Bible is wrong if he despises his brother who, though ignorant of the sacred text, is docile in his faith. It is on the same Word of God that both, in the measure of their charity, live.

(*b*) *It is not forbidden.* Contrary to a "widespread prejudice" (deplored by Pius XII in *Divino Afflante Spiritu*), the Church has never prohibited the ordinary layman from reading the Bible, nor has she forbidden the translation of the sacred books into the vernacular. No authentic document supports such a proposition. The Church simply demands that translations intended for the use of the faithful possess the guarantees of fidelity and intelligibility which her *imprimatur* confirms.[2]

(*c*) *It is recommended.* To all Christians—though with a great deal more urgency, to be sure, to those whose mission it is to teach. This recommendation, rather this insistence, is to be heard throughout the Church's history. If we wished to hear, in a single quotation, the echo of the early centuries and of the magisterium today, we would recall St. Jerome's phrase, which Pius XII adopted as his own at the end of *Divino Afflante Spiritu:* "To be ignorant of the Scriptures is to be ignorant of Christ."

[2] *Codex Iuris Canonici,* can. 1391.

16

This *rapprochement* between the Scriptures and Christ makes clearer the precise nature of the "recommendation" to read the Bible: Frequent recourse to the Scriptures is not suggested as a "luxury" but much more as the normal condition for growth in Christ. In order not to be cut off from His Body, it is "sufficient" to take communion once a year. Certain exalted souls may manifest by a holy life the power of this single communion, but the normal inclination of a fervent and unhampered Christian life is still towards frequent communion. Similarly, it is sufficient (see §*a*), in order to remain within the faith, to adhere to the basic teaching of the Church (and illiterates are not excluded from the most sublime contemplation of the mysteries of God); but the normal inclination of a faith which grows in awareness is to go to the Word of God in its original key. In point of fact, just as the need for the Body of Christ is a sign of spiritual health, so the appetite for the Word of God, in the individual Christian as in the Christian community, is the sign of greater or lesser vitality in the faith.

To this essential consideration, we may add two others which are, we know, quite secondary but still not completely insignificant.

1. Christian life generally becomes *boring* in the very measure in which it thinks it has to remain at a distance from its own well-springs: Bible, liturgy, sacraments, ecclesial community. A Christianity separated from the Bible, a Christianity prepared in readily digestible doses for busy people, or diluted into a regulated infusion of sugared water for the delicate, will be able to sustain a puny sort of life, but it will not bestow that *spiritualis pinguedo* which comes only from divine nourishment. Manuals of dogma, manuals of morality, colleges, private schools, indeed

the very methods of spirituality are capable of maintaining minds in orthodoxy and souls in virtue, but the living Word of God will bestow joy: for tap-water is drinkable, but spring-water refreshes.

2. This vital contact with Christian sources, the Bible in particular, is a necessary condition for the existence of a Christian *culture* or for the understanding of the monuments of that culture. And this includes not only those works which are properly sacred (the liturgical texts, first of all), but also those works of literature and art which were brought forth on Christian soil. For theirs is a witness to a biblical memory and a biblical sensitivity which will only be relished in their fullness by one who is personally familiar with Scripture.

II.

Living Water
and the Wilderness

THE Christian, then, opens his Bible. What does he find there? We can, perhaps, summarize the experience of many by saying that the Bible leads them to two apparently contradictory discoveries:

(*a*) The first is the discovery of living water which, at countless places in the sacred text, spontaneously slakes one's thirst. At some time or other, the Bible speaks to every Christian just as it once spoke to St. Augustine when he listened to the far-off *tolle et lege,* or as it spoke to St. Francis of Assisi when he heard the liturgical reading of the passage which counsels against having two tunics. At times like these, the Bible speaks to us as something which was written just for us and can be understood without commentary. In such a text, the basic instinct of faith is immediately aware of the transcendence of the Word *of God;* the voice never heard before and yet familiar. And in such a text, without any extra effort, we find what concerns *us,* we find the "mirror," as St. James says (1, 22), in which we see "the face that we were born with"—and the face with which we were reborn. This direct and fruitful understanding is ultimately what we

19

are looking for in all our efforts. This is what we are looking for, not just in certain passages or at certain special moments, but wherever God has spoken—all through the Bible—
and whenever we open it. The purpose of the following study
is to see whether this is possible and, if it is, how. No matter
what the outcome of our study, of course, the Bible will never
cease to be the preserve of such free and unexpected meetings.
What we must do is faithfully to distill their grace and, whenever
other parts of the Bible strike us as arid, return to the "bubbling
springs" where we have quenched our thirst before and may
quench it once again. We begin by sketching the map and then
carefully enhance its beauty by recording each new discovery.
The map will be different for everyone. It will, no doubt, show
more detail in the areas which are closest to Jesus: the Gospels,
St. Paul, St. John. But there will be loveliness too from the
Psalms, the prophets, Job, the texts uncovered for us by their
use in the liturgy. To the persevering reader, even the historical
and sapiential books at length reveal their still more hidden
streams.

(b) The second discovery we make is of the "wilderness" of
the Bible, one very much like "that great and terrible wilderness"
(Deut.) which had to be crossed before entering the Promised
Land. It is a wilderness where progress is slow and painful,
where a thousand dangers lurk, where we must dig deep even
to find brackish water, where we soon begin to murmur, a
desert wilderness where mirages suddenly rise up before us.

Reading the Bible raises, then, a great number of questions.
When the reader sees that he is unable to resolve them, or even
clearly to recognize their importance, the difficulties become so
many obstacles on his path. This is the reason why many Chris-

tians become discouraged after they have read the Bible for a little while. It is also the reason why others, with a bit more boldness but no more understanding, think they can rely on their own lights whenever difficulties appear; they end up by interpreting Scripture without rhyme or reason. It might be useful to run through a few of these difficulties.

1. The *meaning* of the text is, after all, often obscure on a first reading. St. Paul's logic of paradox, Revelation's visions and their ramifications, some of the key-words in St. John, many prophetic oracles and their proximate or final perspectives do not yield their message straightway. Even the most obvious texts in the Gospels have a somewhat obscure background: certain phrases ("the kingdom of heaven," "the Son of man") somehow suggest a precision or wealth of meaning which our understanding does not exhaust. And so we find ourselves poring over notes added by a more or less competent translator to the bottom of the page. Or, if we are a bit more sophisticated, we thumb through a concordance. Whether we like it or not, faith demands that we devote our minds to this bare minimum of preliminary effort, if we are ever to grasp the Word of God.

2. Nor is the mind's work finished yet. Now we find it questioning the *truth* of the Bible, asking all sorts of "critical" questions, questions which even the most docile faith cannot suppress. Suppose that we are reading the first three Gospels. There seem to be both striking similarities and just as striking differences. Where do they come from, and what is their common root? We are meeting up with the "synoptic problem." Now suppose that we are reading St. John. The differences, both of substance and of style, between his Gospel and the other three leap up before

21

us and we find ourselves confronted with the "Johannine problem." These are just a few of the questions which *the Bible itself*
presents. Other questions are suggested by the comparison between the Bible and the fruits of secular learning, questions like
the age of the world and the age of man—which, as scholars
see them, are far longer than indicated by the letter, or rather
the chronologies, of Genesis—not to speak of the other problems
presented by the first chapters of that particular book.

A few examples like these should be enough to provoke a
world of questions, which we cannot dispose of simply by calling
them "curious" and then repressing them as "doubts against
faith." They have, to be sure, been used in the past as weapons
for unbelief, and they can so be used again, but it is perfectly
normal for these questions to occur to the Christian as well. The
Fathers of the Church were familiar with them and argued about
them. If we, in our turn, find a way of answering them, we are
by no means throwing doubt on our own position, nor are we
even "defending" our faith. What we are doing is, rather, clear-
ing a way before it and making sure that it discerns its object:
what the Word of God teaches, more exactly and thus more
"faithfully."

3. What is more, the Bible-reading Christian soon discovers
that the *real* difficulties begin when the preliminary obstacles
have been cleared away, and he finds himself at last confronted
with the Bible as the Word of God and clearly sees in it "what
God has said." These difficulties actually stem from the nature
of faith itself, from the radical disproportion between our created
spirit and the mystery of God. While God is simple, we are com-
plex, and until we can see Him face to face, God reveals Himself
to us according to our complexity: in the multiplicity of the

"articles of faith" and in the "economy" of biblical revelation. This is something to which we shall return. For the moment, though, it is sufficient for us thoroughly to grasp the fact that faith, unlike vision, cannot bring rest, and still less slumber, to the spirit. Our knowledge is full of enigmas, and our ambition is to break through them. Here we have the root of the agitation, "the cogitation of faith" which St. Thomas Aquinas spoke of, and which is the beginning of "theology." This is the reason why every Christian is a practicing theologian to the extent that his faith is living and thus is "asking questions." The Christian who reads the Bible in a spirit of faith cannot possibly help encountering new questions, *theological* difficulties every step along the way.

There is some light to be had from the experience of the biblical witnesses themselves. The Twelve, in their daily "conversation" with Christ, actually touched the Man-God. But the things that made an impression on their senses and on their minds were either the patent indications, the "arguments" of His humanity: fatigue, sleep, agony, death; or the dazzling light of His divinity: the sea becalmed, the brilliance on Tabor, the presence of the Risen Lord. Their question was inevitable: "Who then is this?" (Mk. 4, 41), and it never ceased to trouble their faith as they groped along to the confession of the mystery of Christ: "You are the Christ, the Son of the living God." — "My Lord and my God!"

The Bible reveals God and God's works to us too. But it does so in the course of a long story which is made up of *human* words and actions. The transcendence of God is at times hidden and at times obvious, but it is always there. Sometimes we see His mercy, sometimes His justice—indeed, His "injustice." Sometimes we see the imperious demands which His holiness makes, and at other times we see the middling sort of "preparations" through which He is constantly leading His people. The Bible-reading Christian, seeking "the face of God," has a long journey ahead of him, a journey which asks of him an intensely personal redoing, article by article, of his apprenticeship in the faith.

4. It will even seem to him at times that the way he must follow gets lost in the sands. What we have in mind are texts which have apparently nothing whatever to say to the religious soul: the genealogies, the interminable lists, the itineraries, the topographical notes, the legal provisions and the juridical minutiae, the architects' estimates and the details of dress, all of them "burdening" so many pages of Genesis, Exodus, or Leviticus, the sort of thing we are sorely tempted to skip over as extrinsic to our search for God—pretty much as we used to skip over the "instructive" passages in Jules Verne when, as children, we were eager to get on with the story. We are also thinking of a number of other texts which are actually rather entertaining, but are seemingly short on spiritual substance: all those moderately edifying anecdotes in Genesis, Judges, Samuel, and Kings: so much evidence of elementary morality; so many maxims drawn from thoroughly human wisdom which, whether from Proverbs or from Sirach, could with the greatest ease have come from some bourgeois moralist. Aren't passages like these every bit as ill-suited for the purposes of spiritual reading?

They certainly would be, if we limited ourselves to the "flabby breasts of the literal sense" (Claudel) and refused to take into account the fact that they could be concealing a hidden teaching. But this brings us to another problem: that of the *senses* of Scripture.

24

5. Actually, the problem is wider in scope. It is not solely as a means of drawing spiritual profit from dry texts that we search for the hidden meaning, but also as the approach which is best-adapted to one of the characteristics of biblical texts in general: their signification of something more than their immediate content. Let us quote from Claudel once again. "What we do with the texts of Scripture is not what we choose, however much we may try to limit them to the literal sense, to neutralize them. . . . They suddenly start to ferment, to work actively from within, and the old container is all set to burst."

But may it not be true that this superabundance of "spiritual senses" is little more than a mirage, just another product of our imagination? The fact of the matter is, of course, that the majority of the Fathers of the Church, the majority of the mystics, cultivated these "senses." And there are examples everywhere to be found in the liturgy, in the use which is made of biblical texts for common prayer. The more satisfactory conclusion is that the Word of God is truly inexhaustible, that everything in it, quite apart from the limitations imposed by the immediate signification, contains an allusion to the whole of the mystery from which it springs, and that this Word must become for us too—provided we do not stifle the Spirit—not only living water but a *spring* of living water, welling up to eternal life (Jn. 4, 14; 7, 37-39).

Questions like these are some, even though not all, of those suggested by the reading of the Bible. "I thank thee, Father, Lord of heaven and earth, that thou hast hidden these things from the wise and understanding and revealed them to babes" (Mt. 11, 25). And yet we do have the sciences of criticism and theology. As accompaniment for the single note, we have the elaborate counterpoint of commentaries, scholarly or lyrical, minutiae- or mystically-minded. The Bible-reading Christian pauses to catch his breath. We shall pause with him to retrace our steps a bit and isolate a few "principles."

III.

Some Principles for Understanding Scripture

WHEN the believer tries to unravel the skein of questions presented to him as he reads the Bible, he does not stand alone. The Church had already been given the Scriptures as a deposit. And men within the Church have devoted their lives and their labors to the cause of understanding them. The Church is able to offer us the aid of our brothers in the faith through her own maternal magisterium. We hope to be able to take both elements into account. One of them is, to be sure, more important than the other: the Bible in the faith of the Church, and the Bible's self-revelation when it is honestly studied by believing readers. Even though faith is unchanging, research is constantly moving forward. We shall, therefore, ask for the light of the unchangeable reality of faith, which the Church has never ceased to affirm. But we will also recognize that the last half-century's progress in biblical studies and in theological reflection on them has made it possible for us to show in greater detail how that light, so ancient and so new, illumines the questions which occupy our attention today.

1. THE BIBLE, WORD OF GOD AND HUMAN WORD

The Bible is the Word of God. This is what the Bible tells us (2 Tim. 3, 16; 2 Pet. 1, 21), and the Church believes that this is so. The Scriptures are "inspired" by God, by the Holy Spirit. As such, they have God for their "author." It was He who "dictated" them to the inspired writers, thereby making of them His "lyres," His "mouthpieces." This is how the Fathers spoke and the Councils defined. The Council of Florence, for example, proclaimed that "one and the same God is the author of the Old and of the New Testament—the Law and the prophets and the Gospel—because it was under the inspiration of the same Holy Spirit that the holy men of both testaments spoke."[1] The First Vatican Council declared that the books of both testaments, in their entirety, "written under the inspiration of the Holy Spirit, have God for their author."[2]

But the Bible, as is perfectly plain, is a human word as well. It was written in human language, whether Hebrew or Greek, at a particular period in history, and it was written by men (whether we know their names or not) and for men.

In saying that this book, a man's work, is the Word of God and has God for its author, we are expressing the *mystery* of the Bible. It is a mystery analogous to the mystery of the incarnation and is a kind of preparation for it: "God spoke of old to our fathers by the prophets; but in these last days he has spoken to us by a Son" (Heb. 1, 1). It is, then, a mystery which cannot be better explained than by relating it to the mystery of the incarnation. For these five words from the Creed: "who

[1] Denzinger, no. 706.
[2] *Ibid.*, no. 1787.

spoke through the prophets," are an echo of words which have preceded: "and was made man."

"Who spoke." The Bible is the Word of God

For there would be no Bible unless there had been a "revelation," unless, before there was any text, there had been a divine initiative: God speaking to us to let us know about His knowledge and His will. 1 Cor. 2, 11–12: "For what person knows a man's thoughts except the Spirit of God. Now we have received not the spirit of the world, but the Spirit which is from God, that we might understand the gifts bestowed on us by God." The Bible, then, comes from God, from the interior Word which is going to be expressed for us.

Similarly, Jn. 1, 1: "In the beginning was the Word, and the Word was with God, and the Word was God." Christ, then, comes from God.

"Through the prophets." The Bible is Human Word

Revelation, after all, is not man's entry into the vision, by transcending the normal operation of his intelligence. Neither is it an interior word, uncovering for him secrets of a sort which he would not be permitted nor able to lay bare. Revelation, first for the prophet, and then, through him, for us, is expressed in events, gestures, perceptions, concepts, words, all of which are grasped by the senses, imagination, and understanding. Revelation is expressed in human thoughts and words—human, social, communicable, written. This is the first "Incarnation of the Word."

And this is just what we read in Jn. 1, 14: "And the Word became flesh and dwelt among us . . . we have beheld his glory." This is the abasement, the "kenosis," of the Son of God made man.

May we not have here the principle which will clear up many of our difficulties? Anyone who looks at the mystery of the Bible under the light of the mystery of Christ will no longer be astonished by the great number of "too human" questions which Bible-reading provokes. The fact is that the Word of God is presented to us no less humbly than was His Son. "We have *seen*," says St. John, "His glory." What John had heard, seen with his eyes, had looked upon and touched with his hands (1 Jn. 1, 1) was a man—who was "the Word of life." All the human activity had been necessary, the living together, the eating together, the walking together with Him had been necessary so that Peter (and we after him, and linked to him by an unbroken chain of witnesses) could confess "what eye has not seen nor ear heard," what "flesh and blood has not revealed": "You are the Christ, the Son of the living God." In like manner, *this* human activity is necessary—the hearing of the words communicated, the reading of a book written by a man's hand, and the unremitting effort to understand it—if we are to lay hold of the Word of God.

2. THE INSPIRATION OF HOLY SCRIPTURE

"Inspiration" is the mysterious bond between the divine and the human in the Bible. If we wish to define it properly, we must be on our guard against two errors, analogous, once again, to the two errors which lie along the path of true knowledge of Christ:

1. There are many who, knowing Jesus "too well," refuse to believe in Him: "Is not this the carpenter's son?" — "We know

where this man comes from; and when the Christ appears, no one will know where He comes from."

And in just the same way will it be said, after the Bible has been carefully read, analyzed, and commented upon: Here is a book which is the work of man. The very text of the Bible, when closely studied, reveals a number of authors, succeeding one another, contradicting one another, correcting one another. Their way of thinking is the product of their age—its milieu, its preoccupations, its doubts. They worked on documents which were already in existence when they began. We can detect what influenced them. We can find resemblances and even parallel passages in the secular writings of their age. Such is the position of the rationalist critics of the Bible. If we are to make this a Christian position, it will not be enough for us to say that God aided—as from the outside—this human effort, so as to preserve it from error, and therefore that His authority imposes it on our faith. This is not the way to give full meaning to what the Church affirms: the Bible has God for its *author*.

2. When the approach of the passion was announced, Peter said, "God forbid, Lord! This shall never happen to you." He had already forgotten the mortal humanity "even unto death on the cross" of Him whose divinity he had just confessed. And, in point of fact, the first Christological heresy was *Docetism,* which refused, through various artifices, to admit that the Son of God was also the Crucified.

Similarly, some of us can be tempted into a kind of "biblical Docetism." Strong on the dogmatic formula "God is the author of the Bible" and convinced of a spiritual experience which permits them to recognize the transcendence of the divine Word under the letter of the text, such readers refuse to see, or to take

31

very seriously, the human and defective elements pointed out by critics. They make of the Bible a direct "dictation" by God to purely passive writers, in precisely the same way as Moslems see the Koran as a work brought forth, just as it is, from the thought of Allah, "uncreated."—But the book of books itself insists upon and witnesses to a "humanity" which is not simply a matter of appearances.

We must, then, "hold on to both ends" and confess, along with the Church,[3] that the inspiration of the Holy Spirit does not exclude the activity of men but assumes it in such a way as to make of the Bible, which has God for its author, a book with human authors *as well*.

To be sure, it is no easy task to express the mystery of this "motion" which, while sovereign, is nonetheless vitally and actively received. We cannot enter at this time into a detailed discussion of the theological controversies which scriptural inspiration has provoked.[4] They are reminiscent of the controversies which sought to bring into focus another mystery: the free and meritorious act of man under the motion of God's

[3] See the following passage from Leo XIII's encyclical *Providentissimus Deus*: "The Holy Spirit stirred up [the sacred writers] and moved them to write; He aided them when they wrote, so that they rightly conceived, intended to write faithfully, and exactly expressed, with an infallible truth, all that He directed them to write and only what He directed them to write: He would not otherwise be the author of the Holy Scriptures in their entirety. . . ." It will be noted that this text, which vigorously demonstrates that the motion of the Holy Spirit was everywhere present in the redaction of Holy Writ, makes use of terms (conceive, intend to write, express) which at the same time suppose activity and real initiative on the part of the inspired writer.

[4] On this question, we would refer the reader to the excellent treatment of St. Thomas Aquinas's tract on inspiration (*Summa Theologica*, IIa–IIae, qq. 171–178) by P. Synave and P. Benoit, *Prophecy and Inspiration* (New York, 1961).

grace. In both instances, there is something which comes from man and *also* comes from God: whether a human act which merits eternal life, or an oracle or book which expresses the Word of God. If we wish to "understand" this, we will undoubtedly do better by avoiding too clearly defined a division or even too distinct a compromise, with this aspect belonging to man and that aspect to God. What we should keep in mind is that one of the relevant terms—the divine action—transcends the other, is the creator of the other, and is therefore able to assume it without destroying it. Everything is man's and everything is God's. God the Creator bestows "life, movement, and being" on everything. Still in all, beings have their own independence, and their causality is not a mere appearance nor a disguise of the First Cause. It is indeed the grace of God which saves, and yet every man is free and must "force" his way into the kingdom to which the Father "draws" him.

In precisely the same way, the divine motion, when exercised on the prophet or biblical writer, "inspires" the entire process of thought and action which leads to the prophetic or written act. And yet that act stems vitally from its human author. There is nothing in the Bible, whether thoughts, images, or words— even "the tail of Tobit's dog"—which escapes divine inspiration. Nor is there anything in the thoughts, images, or words of the Bible which cannot bear, which is not *intended* to bear the mark of the man—his particular genius, his mentality, his era.

How, then, are we to read the Bible? God Himself reads it, if the expression may be permitted me, "over the shoulders" of those whom He inspires. God reads it from the inside. In time, we will too, should He allow us to enter into His glorious intimacy. We will read it "in Him," and then we will see the "mechanics of inspiration" from His point of view. But we have not yet arrived at that stage. What is accessible to us now are the words and the thoughts which our understanding can grasp, and thereby enhance the strength of our faith. We have to *rise* to the crest of inspiration. In order to discover how inspiration works, we have no other course—once we are certain that it is everywhere present—than to seek it in an attitude of humble attention to the letter which is vivified by the spirit.

We cannot undertake to sum up all that is revealed by such a search, both about the Bible itself and about the diversity and complexity of biblical inspiration.[5] Therefore, we shall limit our attention to two points which are of the greatest relevance to the uncertainties or difficulties experienced by the Christian in his reading of Holy Scripture: the variety of "literary genres" and biblical inerrancy.

What is a *literary genre?* Anyone who has glanced through the shelves of a library, large or small, knows quite well. A treatise on mathematics, a historical study, a cookbook, a campaign address, a fairy tale, a drama, a novel all belong to different literary genres. Irrespective of the talent of their authors, they differ as to their ends and as to their means. They differ as to their ends in that they are addressed to different publics, or, within the same public, to different sectors or classes of understanding, sympathy, imagination, or will. They also differ as to the means adapted to those ends: prose or poetry, rigorous

[5] To give but one example, there are distinctions which must be made: (*a*) between inspiration and *revelation* (the inspiration of a biblical author neither necessarily nor always brings him a new "revelation"; it can simply cause him to judge, as God judges, facts and thoughts known humanly by him); (*b*) between inspiration and *authenticity* (the inspiration of a biblical text does not prevent us from seeing, in a proper case, various hands, all of which are subject, in their successive efforts, to that inspiration).

or flamboyant ordering of ideas, preciseness or resonance in the use of language, all depending on whether the end sought is demonstration, conviction, or distraction. And we obviously do not read these books in the same way. *Alice in Wonderland* "bewitches" us. We "bone up" on the *Uniform Commercial Code.*

The Bible also contains a like variety. It has *its* literary genres —and we must be very careful about assimilating them too quickly to literary genres with which we are familiar. The presence of literary genres in the Bible will not surprise us if we have truly understood that the Bible, the Word of God, is a truly human word as well. And we will not consider it a useless effort to investigate the fine points (or the inadequacies) of the literary forms in which God chose to let His witnesses express themselves, if we really want to know "what God has said"— and what is alone important. Neither will we think that we have to treat so great a number of different books in the same way, or read them according to the same criteria. Even if they possess a secret unity (a subject to which we shall return shortly) in God's great design which is expressed in all of them (Pascal speaks, for example, of "digressions" which seem to distract us from the end but actually go right on pointing to it), we still must begin by reading them exactly as they are and giving them the particular kind of attention they demand. In this way, we let ourselves be guided by the Bible itself, and we help each other acquire insights into the Bible's purposes. We learn to distinguish between Luke's style and John's, and we see how the same event in the life of Christ can have a different impact on each. We learn that we cannot read in the same way the story of creation (Gen. 1) and the story of Jesus' death: "And Jesus uttered a loud cry, and breathed his last" (Mk. 15, 36), for we

35

realize that they are different kinds of "history." We do not put Job's outbursts of despairing hope and Sirach's serene and prudent wisdom into the same category. We discern the expressive power of prophetic deeds and words. We seek the "spirit" within the various "mentalities," and do so successfully only in the measure in which we have grasped those mentalities. (And exegetes who are equipped to help us no longer strike us as vain propounders of "curious" questions, but are eagerly embraced as valuable companions.)

As a relevant factor, the literary genre of biblical texts will be of immense aid also when we attempt to discern precisely what the texts, as protected by the gift of "inerrancy," affirm.

Holy Scripture's *inerrancy* follows immediately from its inspiration. God is Truth: He can neither deceive nor be deceived. Since God is, through inspiration, the author of the Bible, the Bible in its turn cannot contain error.

And yet we do have in point of fact, the impression of detecting errors in the biblical text. Even the reader who is least susceptible of being termed "hypercritical" will come across seeming instances of error—unless he reads with a rather sophisticated feeling for the modes of biblical language. He will, for example, come upon two accounts of the same fact, both of which are inspired and yet are divergent. How is such divergence to be explained other than by the error, partial at least, of one or the other?

The answer to questions of this kind is perfectly simple in principle, but no less varied and nuanced in practice. Truth or error is present only when and in the measure that there is an *affirmation*. What we just finished saying about the variety of literary genres suggests that we should be prepared to find corresponding variety in degrees of affirmation and, consequently, in possibilities of truth or error, such as are encountered in human language—and in biblical language. There is a truth proper to mathematics, and a truth proper to history. There is *also* a truth proper to legend, a truth proper to poetry, and a truth proper to a scream in the night. If we expect to give to the content of the biblical expression the faithful adherence which is always demanded of us, we must give our humble attention to the expressions themselves—and they are as varied as man's language and heart. When Ecclesiastes writes (3, 19–20), "The fate of the sons of men and the fate of beasts is the same; as one dies, so dies the other. They all have the same breath, and man has no advantage over the beasts; for all is vanity. All go to one place; all are from the dust, and all turn to dust again," it is the *truth* of the *doubt* which faith must surpass that is being expressed. When Peter declares, "This Jesus God raised us, and of that we all are witnesses" (Acts 2, 32), he states the fact in its raw truth. The truth of the human language in the inspired Bible is indeed guaranteed by the very Truth of God, but the precise "impact" of divine Truth on the truth of the human language—that is, the inerrancy of the Bible—can be properly appreciated only if we have sufficient awareness of the possibilities (and the deficiencies) of that language.

The question can be asked whether we have, throughout this process, remained faithful to the *mystery* of the Bible. This is, after all, the mystery Pius XII called to our attention, after he had set forth the diversity of literary genres in the sacred books. What he said in *Divino Afflante Spiritu* was that "none of the modes of speech which human language customarily used to express thought among the ancients, the Orientals particularly, is foreign to the sacred text, provided, however, that the genre employed is in no sense contrary to the holiness or truth of God," for "just as the substantial Word of God was made like unto men in all things, save sin, so are the words of God, when expressed in human language, error alone excepted." We see the extent to which Pius XII carried our initial analogy between Christ and the Bible.

This alone may be enough to make us suspect that the violent opposition between the "literal" and the "spiritual" reading of Holy Scripture, which some have striven so hard to make inexpiable, simply does not exist. Although it cannot be questioned that there are various ways of reading the Bible, there is still but one *exegesis,* towards which each of the ways is oriented, although it may not completely ignore, and still less despise, the rest. Men must go to Christ by many different routes, but "Christ is not divided."

3. THE MEANING AND THE MEANINGS OF SCRIPTURE

Does Holy Scripture have one or several meanings? Is there a hidden meaning which must be sought under the obvious meaning? And is the "spiritual meaning," of which we have so many examples in the New Testament's quotation of the Old, in the Fathers' commentaries on the sacred text, and in the liturgical use of Scripture in the Church's prayer, one of the real meanings of the Bible, a meaning intended by God who was present to the mind of the biblical writer? And where does this spiritual meaning begin? Where does it end? What we have already said about the Bible's human language and about

38

the economy of sacred history[6] makes it possible for us to see this problem in a clearer light.

We begin with a few common-sense considerations (common sense still makes the best marriage with mystery).

The text of a passage, when carefully written and completely honest, denotes a reality which the passage seeks to make known, and it denotes only one: it has *a* meaning. There are only two cases where a passage can have several meanings. The first is where an author "stammers" and fails to find the proper word. The second is where a dishonest author intentionally uses ambiguous language so as to deceive his public. Both cases are obviously excluded from the inspired books, whose authors were aided by the Holy Spirit to express themselves accurately ("suitably," as the encyclical *Providentissimus Deus* puts it). Besides, it would be repugnant to the Truth of God to deceive deliberately. On occasions, God can, of course, tell us difficult things in language which is difficult to understand, but He cannot purposely send us down the wrong road by telling us what Péguy called "twaddle."

If, then, we keep to the text of the Bible, and to what the inspired author intended to say and did say, we see that the Bible has one *literal* meaning and no more than one.

We will not lose sight of the multiplicity of "literary genres" used by the Bible, but we will certainly avoid too ready an identification of the literal meaning with the superficial meaning yielded by mere "grammatical analysis" of phrases. This, of

[6] We have attempted to develop these points in our treatment of Oscar Cullmann's beautiful book, *Christ and Time* (Philadelphia, 1950), which, even if it does not give a completely satisfactory solution to the problem of sacred history, at least presents it in absolutely scriptural terms. See our *Approaches to a Theology of History*, New York, 1965, pp. 5–40.

course, is a rule which we make use of daily, for it is relevant to all human language. When we read in Corneille, for example: "Go, I hate thee not at all," we know perfectly well that this hesitant way of speaking means ("literally") something quite different from what we would suspect if we came to it armed only with a dictionary and ignorant of the context. In the Bible, too, the *literal* meaning can be figurative (as in a parable in the Gospels), it can be ironic, it can conceal allusions. It can be the meaning of a story, or of a question, or of an order, or of a prayer. It can, finally, state a reality which is properly inexpressible and which it denotes rather than contains. "Literal meaning," then, is not synonymous with "immediately intelligible meaning," nor with "meaning bereft of spiritual content." The "literal meaning" can be quite difficult, and it can also possess a richness which is not immediately perceived.

Once we have discovered this "literal meaning," with or without difficulty, can we say that we have exhausted the "understanding" of the Bible? *Intelligere*—understanding something— is derived from *intus* and *legere,* "to read within." Where the text is a written one, *intelligere* means grasping the reality through the text, "under" the text. And it is the literal meaning which does this for us. It is possible, however, that this particular reality is itself related to another, which it prepares for, signifies, makes us think of. When we grasp, in a new thrust of the mind, the relationship between reality "1," of which we read in the text, and reality "2," we are discovering within the text itself a *second meaning*—for in that text we are also reading reality "2." This is a "spiritual" meaning (if we choose to use that expression) in that the second reality is itself spiritual—but let us not forget that the first reality can be spiritual too—, and also because the bond which unites it to the first is a spiritual bond. If the second meaning is to be other than an arbitrary notion, the bond must be real.

Now—and here we see the mystery and transcendence of the Bible as compared with every other human book—this kind of bond actually exists between the various realities which the letter of the Bible teaches us in many and various ways, *multifariam multisque modis*. So as to recognize the legitimacy of the spiritual meaning and to establish limitations for it, we should remember that the Bible is sacred history. As history, it tells us of a thousand happenings, puts forward a thousand thoughts, and each has its own date and sphere of influence—the literal meaning makes us see them for what they are. But as sacred history, guided throughout by God who transcends the limitations of time, it is "cut from a single piece," it is going somewhere, and in its totality it has a meaning. It is certain, therefore, that an immense spiritual meaning holds sway throughout the sacred text. By putting each happening or each thought in its *total* context— not merely in the context of a particular book, but in the context of the "economy" of a revelation whose every deed and whose every inspired word is just a fragment—, that meaning gives the happening or thought, when seen with the eyes of faith, a meaning which is pregnant with the future, gives it an "eternal weight of glory."

To the question whether this general spiritual meaning takes on greater precision in more particular spiritual meanings, the answer is yes. At the heart of the economy of revelation, more immediate relationships (preparation, prefiguring) exist between certain elements, and these relationships can be more immediate than revelation itself implies or we can infer. One could speak of the structure of sacred history and of the Bible as "fibrous," since it allows us to see within it all sorts of currents, kinships, and calls. Péguy wrote that everything happens "three times" in Christianity: in the Old Testament, in Christ, and in His saints. It would be more exact to say that correlations, "figures," are to be found as between the Old Testament and the New, Christ's New Testament and Christians, and the "whole" Christ in His present condition and in that of the age to come. And the reason for this is that a causality, a "preparation" exists.

In recognizing these correlations, we find the spiritual or "typical" meaning of a given passage from Scripture. This meaning not only can but will be threefold (assuming that we succeed in following the "fibers" through to the end): "Christic," in showing the reference to Christ or to the New Testament in a given passage from the Old Testament; "tropological" or "moral" (to use terms which, though improper, are traditional), in showing how the life of the Christian (especially in its *sacramental* reproduction of the life of Christ) can be seen in a given prior event or instruction; and "anagogical," in perceiving therein a forecast of the characteristics of the kingdom which is to come. Thus the passage (the "passover") of the Hebrews through the Red Sea, their "baptism" in water and fire, both prepares for and prefigures: the Christian passover, which is the death and resurrection of Christ; the Christian passover as reproduced in Christian baptism; and finally the passage from this world to the next in the parousia of the Lord.

But is that what the author of Exodus meant? Clearly not, if we were obliged to infer from "meant" that he was thinking of such clearly defined correlations. At all events, he said nothing about them, and we have no justification for introducing them into the literal meaning. But, as he narrated the events which took place at the Red Sea, he was undoubtedly thinking—and his text surely suggests the spiritual reality—of a *total* salvation, a decisive event for Israel which would have a definitive impact on its history; it is beside the point that he might have viewed this salvation in merely carnal perspectives. The prophets and the Psalms, as they meditate on Exodus, will develop the spiritual significance. When we, in turn, look back towards our origins, we can see that what then began in carnal fashion is the *same* operation of passing-over, breach, triumphant traversing of death which God accomplished in the pasch of Christ and began anew in us. The continuity was affirmed in the clearest possible way by Jesus Himself, when He placed the new pasch within the framework of the celebration of the old (Lk. 22; Mk. 14; Mt. 26), a point which is emphasized by texts like 1 Cor. 10. This is an example of a spiritual meaning with an undeniable double foundation: it is based on the literal meaning of Exodus, on the reality of the facts which Exodus recounts; and it surpasses that meaning because of a solid bond between the reality of those facts and another reality. The later rich development of this theme by the Fathers and the liturgy (in the *Exultet* of the paschal vigil, for example) has, therefore, a perfectly sound premise from which to start. We find that we are completely within the spiritual meaning *of* Scripture.

We are not always on such solid ground. Although we are more or less aware, before we start to read, that everything in the Bible should be seen in perspective, certain details of the perspective are occasionally "off-center," as other texts of Scripture or the formal teaching of the Church would show. Most of the time, the details are left to our own investigation, through which we can go astray. Then too, it is unquestionable that the spiritual meaning of many texts is a simple absence of such meaning, and consists merely in carrying forward the humble historical thread of a drama in which there are "walk-ons" and "bit-parts." Tobit's dog surely does not wag its tail (Tob. 11, 9) for the purpose of announcing a mystery—if the story-teller makes it a part of his tale, his sole intention is most likely to entertain us (yet even this intention can occasion some useful reflection on the human quality of the Word of God). And there are minor episodes in the historical books whose spiritual significance, while still a real one, is merely to remind us that salvation is a reality and that its history can have a wearisome character. Other passages have a clearly open perspective, a "fibre." But when we undertake to set forth precisely the relationship which we suspect to exist between the reality asserted in the text and the far-off or hidden realities connected with it, we risk introducing, on our own, *rapprochements* which are ill-advised, details which are arbitrary, notions which are childish. Even the Fathers were more or less consciously guilty of this sort of thing, and occasionally corrected their own excesses with the touch of humor which can save us from our own cleverness.

The road which has led us from the "literal" meaning (the only meaning sought by the human author) to the "spiritual" meaning is thus apparent. It now leads us from the real spiritual meaning (the meaning which rests on a real relationship, one which is itself revealed within two revealed realities and is therefore a "scriptural meaning") to the so-called "accommodated" meaning (which is not a "scriptural meaning"). The latter implies a personal contribution by the commentator, and stands or falls on his intelligence, imagination, taste, and Christian feeling. Such free interpretations can, of course, be quite close to the real spiritual meaning. They can also have but a slender connection with it. They can run over into pure fantasy, and can even be utter misconceptions of the real spiritual meaning.

What are we to think of these "meanings"? The theologians and the "factual-minded" will arch their eyebrows. They will rightly warn against the dangers of abuse and will remind us that this is not the meaning of the Bible. But they will themselves be wrong in condemning, for instance, the use so freely made of these "meanings" by the Church in her liturgical prayer, and even in putting an absolute prohibition on the Christian's freedom of interpretation (which obviously should stop short of ascribing fantasies to the Holy Spirit). The house of God, after all, is not a museum filled with "Do Not Touch" signs. It is the house of our Father and it is made to give shelter to men's lives— and to children's games.

But what the difficulties connected with the interpretation of the meanings of Scripture show better than anything else is the vital importance of a last "principle": the bond between Scripture and the Church.

4. SCRIPTURE AND TRADITION

When we say that the Bible is the book of the Church, we are actually reasserting that the Bible is a sacred history. For a history assumes the existence of a *people* and belongs to them, and they alone can understand it—quite differently from historians. Sacred history is the history of the "people of God." In the measure that we belong to that people, the Bible becomes *our* history and has something to say to us.

Moses spoke with God "as friend to friend"; St. Paul was caught up to the third heaven, where secrets were revealed to him "which man may not utter." But this divine intimacy, this life alone with God, was not the reason why the Word of God sought them out. Moses and Paul were sought out for the benefit of the people, the people with whom Moses was burdened from Sinai on, the people whose mystical identity with Christ Paul learned on the road to Damascus: "I am Jesus, whom you are persecuting." None of the witnesses of the Old and New Testaments received his message except for the people of God. Consequently, no reader can understand their message unless he is *within* the people of God—within the Church.

The relationship between the Bible and the Church consists precisely in the following points:

1. It is inexact to oppose or even to juxtapose Scripture and Tradition, as if they constituted "two" sources of revelation, extrinsic to one another. It is more accurate to say that Tradition comprehends Scripture (in every sense of the word "comprehend"). For the Word of God, before it was set down in writing, began by summoning a living people into existence (and the Church is this people in their spiritual realization). The Word of God was entrusted to this people, whose living Tradition it became (guaranteed by the aid of the Holy Spirit). Within this living Tradition, the Word of God assumed a particular (and privileged, because of scriptural inspiration) expression in Scripture. No text—not even the sacred text—stands between the living Word of God and the life which proceeds from it within the Church. And it is *within* the Church—which is living—that Scripture too exists, not as a dead "letter," but as "spirit."

2. Consequently, the Church is *Verbi divini custos et magistra*, guardian and teacher of the Word of God. As particularly regards Scripture, this means: —that the Church "guards" Scripture by establishing its "canon," by determining, in definitive and infallible fashion, which books are inspired; —that the Church, "teacher" of this Word, is alone equipped to *determine* its ultimate meaning, that is, not to make it up, but to recognize

46

it just as God inspired it.[7] For, as St. Irenaeus wrote, "where the Church is, there is the Spirit of God"; and only where the Spirit of God is can we understand what the Spirit of God has inspired.

This authentic interpretation of Scripture has several modes of expression: either the explicit declaration of the meaning of a given passage by the extraordinary and infallible magisterium (this is an extremely rare case; an example of it is the "realist" interpretation of the "This is my body" by the Council of Trent); or the unanimous opinion of the Fathers and Doctors of the Church (which can rarely be established with certainty); or (and this is the usual case) the ordinary teaching of the Church in matters of faith and morals—which provides us with the general framework within which we must understand Scripture.

3. The practical consequence of all this for the Bible-reading Christian is that he must never think of himself as *alone* when he is reading the Bible. This bit of advice has two meanings: one is warning, and the other is encouragement. Warning: Reading the Bible is not meant to be a substitute for ordinary instruction (our catechism and the sermons of our pastor), for prayer together and sacramental life, for community in charity—cut off from these foundations, our Bible-reading produces no understanding and may even lead to a distorted understanding. Encouragement: Linked as we are to the Body, we can count on the aid of the Spirit, and our own humble efforts will profit the entire Body.

[7] See Vatican I (Denzinger, no. 1788): "The true meaning of Holy Scripture must be held to be the meaning which is held and has been held by Holy Mother Church, whose mission it is to judge the true meaning and interpretation of the Holy Scriptures."

We see, then, that only the Church is in the same class as the Bible, and only she has the greatness of heart to "comprehend" the Word which surpasses the natural and supernatural capacities of her children. Still in all, each of her children contributes in his own way to the fervor of her own meditation on the Bible. Thus it was with the events of the first Christmas. There were several witnesses, all more or less well-informed, but Mary—the figure of the Church—"kept all these things, pondering them in her heart" (Lk. 2, 19). In the Church, "there are varieties of gifts, but the same Spirit" (1 Cor. 12, 4). With the assistance of all these gifts, the Church reads, understands, and lives the inspired Word: the learning of the exegetes, the faith of the Fathers and theologians, the prayer of the *opus Dei,* the love of the saints, the imagination of the poets, the shapes and colors of the Bibles in stone and oil . . . There are "various ways of reading the Bible," and no single way is sufficient, nor is any way superfluous.

IV.

Various Ways of Reading
the Bible

We shall limit ourself to a concise outline. It should be apparent that the various "ways" are differentiated and contrasted solely for increased clarity. As a matter of fact, anyone who accepts the guidance of the Bible, of the Spirit, and of the Church, will invariably adopt these different approaches in some order or other, passing now from this to that, and at times combining them.

(a) *Consecutive* reading. Why shouldn't we read the Bible as we would read any other book? We can adopt the approach of the traveler who wishes to learn more about a new country but, rather than doing a lot of business or making a lot of inquiries, rather than checking up on guides and statistics, begins just by strolling along looking at the countryside. This type of reading will reveal a great deal. It will also suggest a good many questions, to which the answers will come later on. It rules out neither curiosity nor religious feeling nor the effort to understand, but it does rule out the pretension of understanding everything. And it finds its needed development in the other ways of reading.

(b) *"Critical"* reading. This means the effort to understand, the effort to arrive at the "literal meaning." While it is, of course, an effort of reason, it is nonetheless oriented and controlled by faith. What it demands is an understanding of the original text (or a good translation) and also a "sense of context." As to the latter, the familiarity acquired during the "consecutive reading" will be a big help. It will not be enough, however, for there are many difficulties—historical, literary, etc.—which will require the average Christian to seek the aid of competent guides.

(c) *Liturgical* reading. For many of the faithful, this will be the first reading. By reading the Bible as we pray with the Church, we find in it a threefold benefit: we relive, during the course of the liturgical year, sacred history and relive it as *our own;* we penetrate, precisely through our prayer, the exact theological meaning of revelation; we acquire, through the unrestrainedly "spiritual" use which the liturgy makes of biblical texts, a certain feeling for allusions, correlations, resonances.

(d) *Theological* reading. This reading is the work of faith seeking knowledge, faith explicitly seeking the Word of God in the Bible so as better to understand what it reveals to us. This reading actually begins with (a) and (b), and especially with (c), but is here pursued for its own sake. It leads us to return to our reading of the text so as to determine, for example, what the Old and the New Testament teach us about God, the Trinity, grace . . .

(e) *Spiritual* reading. We have already been introduced to this kind of reading, particularly by (c) and (d). Indeed, our personal meditation could not dispense with the liturgical or theological reading of the Bible without running considerable risk. Still, there comes a moment when the voice of the believing intellect and the very voice of the Church grow silent and let me hear what the Bible has to say to me alone. After we have put in a few hours of Bible study, or have sung the psalmody of the Divine Office, we simply have to read the Bible in reverent silence, as did St. Thérèse of Lisieux or Père de Foucauld. It then becomes the irreplaceable food of life in God.

(*f*) "*Poetic*" reading. This is something extra, the increase that comes with the gifts of God. This is where the Bible unlocks our store of dreams and song and stimulates all sorts of imaginative and expressive powers, lyrical, dramatic, artistic, whether in painting, sculpture, or in dance. Wisdom freely takes its delight with the children of men, and we need only partake with joy when the grace of the game is given us. The only rules are the "rules of the game": familiarity mingled with reverence and love's delicate reserve. It is then that the Bible becomes, as Claudel says, "the book of adoration," "the book of wonder."

We see, then, that there are *several* ways of reading the Bible, and not just one. Nor is any one of these ways imposed on any of us in just the same fashion. The ways variously correspond with various abilities, vocations, and missions. But no one of them can do without the others, and no one of them can be the particular preserve of any one person. Each of us must make use of the gifts that are his, but within the Church and for the benefit of his brethren, "for God is not a God of confusion but of peace" (1 Cor. 14, 33).

SECOND PART

THE SWORD AND THE WORD

Simple Thoughts to Nourish Our Faith

I.

The Bible is a Sacred History

THE Bible is the Word of God. What we must do now is to give our attention to another aspect of this Word. It does not reveal to us God's eternal "nature" (as certain philosophers, forgetting their condition in time, have dreamed of contemplating) in ready-made fashion, but tells us the story of God's *temporal* intervention in our own human history. God brings about our entry into His eternity only by entering into our history Himself. Our God, the God of the Bible, is not "the God of the philosophers and the learned," but "the God of Abraham, of Isaac, and of Jacob." One more consequence of the mystery of the incarnation, in which the Bible participates.

The first verse of St. John's Gospel is phrased in the imperfect tense, indicative of eternity: "In the beginning was the Word, and the Word was with God, and the Word was God" (ἦν). But the text goes on to say (1, 14), "And the Word became flesh," and it here employs the "historical" past tense (ἐγένετο). Thus does the eternal Word of God move into history. In our Creed, there is a reference to a specific time: "under Pontius Pilate." And the Bible itself is a history.

But it is a *sacred* history, a history, that is to say, whose protagonist is "*the Eternal*," in just the same way as a *human* word is the Word *of God*. A history in which God acts disconcerts us just as much as a human language by which God expresses Himself. Here again, we must hold on to both ends of a chain which is linked together by the mystery of "the economy"—a mystery analogous to that of inspiration.

A history. We can, therefore, expect to find in the Bible something other than pure and timeless "ideas." Neither will we find "myths" in which the idea is masked within an artificial framework. Nor will we find "dialectical moments" in which facts lose their stark reality by becoming part of a logic which both directs and surpasses them. What we will find are *events* or, to speak more precisely, "various facts" (such as the fact which, in Acts 25, 18–19, seemed so devoid of interest to Porcius Festus the governor: "one Jesus, who was dead, but whom Paul asserted to be alive"). We read about cities being founded, about peoples in migration, about battles—and also about simple human happenings: about men who live and die. What we read about are all things which happen only once, which resist any logic, which are spread out along the river of time—whose flow is irreversible and whose courses are unsurmountable . . .

But a sacred history. A history whose every event marks an intervention of God, of "the Eternal," in time, so that each event acquires an importance for *all* time, though without exceeding either its own limitations or its temporal condition: each event reveals God, and brings about the forward passage of salvation. There is still more to be said: the *central* event—which is the Word made flesh—mysteriously brings together all these scattered events into a single history, organizing them into an "economy." When St. Paul recalls the events which occurred in the desert and the "spiritual" rock where the Israelites quenched their thirst, he can add (1 Cor. 10, 1–6): "and the Rock was Christ." "The Rock was Christ," because the event which took place in the desert was itself part of the forward movement, driven on by a force which surpasses time and for which "a thousand years are as a day," towards the Easter event, and was destined to find, in that event, its own true meaning.

If we really want to acquire some understanding of the Bible, therefore, we must not overlook the fact of time, nor God's lordship over time. We would be overlooking the fact of time if we sought to accelerate its passage or to cancel out its distances, if we were to see in the Old Testament, for example, nothing but an imaginative projection of the New—as if events did not possess their own intrinsic consistency, their carnal existence. We would be overlooking the fact of time if we disregarded the slowness, the delays, the back-trackings of the divine preparations; if we let Calvary swallow up the real slopes of Mount Moriah which prefigured it, real slopes which were scaled in measured steps by a flesh-and-blood Abraham and Isaac; if we sought to make Elijah think like St. John of the Cross. Yet we would be overlooking the lordship of God *over* time if we "atomized" sacred history into a dusty train of unconnected events, if we failed to see its "economy"—an economy which implies "theology," the gaze which faith directs towards the mysteries of God which His acts reveal to us.

II.

The Bible is a Promise

The Expectation of Israel

THEY say that a happy people has no history. If this is so, there can be no such thing as a happy people, since all peoples have a history, though historians might fail to write it down. And there can be no such thing as a people which cares particularly about being happy, for the first signs of life among a people are accompanied by a great concern about acquiring a history, the most eventful history possible.

If men and peoples are made for happiness, the simple truth is that happiness is not delivered to them ready-made—we were going to say pre-cooked—for them to take and keep warm. They must *journey* towards happiness, and this journey is history. It is our common fate. Peoples which truly exist as peoples, peoples with a history, do not live in happiness but live rather on hope. Their greatness consists in the character and strength of their hopes.

The People of God has a history, and the Bible recounts it to us. This history also has a hope which drives the people forward on their journey. The hope of the People of God, though, is not like the hope of the peoples of the earth. Even its name is different. It is called "expectation" and it is based not on man's ideas and plans but on the promises of God. The Bible tells the story of these promises and their fulfillment and renewal.

Israel is "the people of the promise." What is it waiting for? A posterity, a Land. The posterity miraculously given to Abraham enters at last into Canaan, the Promised Land. Is this the fulfillment of the promise? No. God is not so quickly relieved of His promises, nor are men so quickly settled in the affluence of God. God's promises are not like man's, to be more or less perfectly realized and all is said and done. The divine promise is not "fulfilled," nor does it even seem to be, except in pushing us ever forward towards a Gift of creative generosity as yet unsuspected by us. This is the course followed by the expectation of Israel, through success and failure, discouragement and revival, from promise to promise, or, better still, deeper and deeper into the unique Promise not at first understood. Behind the stump of David, see the suffering Messiah of Isaiah; beyond the earthly Jerusalem, see that other Jerusalem which the "remnant of Israel" learns to desire by the side of Babylon's waters and on the ruins of the Temple of Solomon; beyond the sufferings of Job, see the hope of a Redeemer who would finally vanquish death. It is then that John the Baptist can appear. And the kingdom of God —which had never seemed so far away—is at hand.

Sacred History is not Finished

"We have found him of whom Moses in the law and also the prophets wrote," says Philip to Nathanael, "Jesus of Nazareth." He goes about doing good, He heals the sick, drives out demons, preaches the Good News to the poor, makes the Old Law burst asunder through the force of new beatitudes, fulfills the passover of Moses by His death and resurrection. In the thirty-third year of our era, the world is saved.

Is this the fulfillment? "Lord, will you at this time restore the kingdom to Israel?" Jesus answers the question only by making His disciples the witnesses of a new period of waiting. The expectation of Israel is followed by the Christian expectation: the return of Christ.

The old life goes on: sin, and death. "In the world you have tribulation." Lazarus who rose from his tomb must return to it again. We must wait, but we do not wait as Israel did, completely turned towards the future. Even now we are touching our goal, we who live in "the last age" and have even now a conclusive sign of final victory: the risen Christ who "will never die again; death no longer has dominion over him." The Gift guarantees the Promise. Christ will return, but He is already reigning. He has already "overcome the world" and we have overcome it with Him. Christ is, for us, "the expectation of Glory."

Towards the Fullness of Christ

What is still lacking? Ourselves. Our effort, our prayer. The whole world must hear the Easter message, and it is our job to see that this is done. Believing in Jesus Christ, we must follow after Him, and, with our brethren, follow the same road which led Him from death to life. "In my flesh," St. Paul says, "I complete what is lacking in Christ's afflictions for the sake of his body, that is, the church." We are men who have not yet arrived at our goal, who are still journeying. There are promises left for us, and we have something still to do in history. Frenchmen sing "The Republic calls us." And the Church calls all Christians. The entire Bible resounds with a call to arms. Another tap on the shoulder! We are needed.

The Church calls us, but her call goes even beyond us. The Church's call to men whom she must bring together in Christ is also a call to Christ Himself, a call for Him to come. It is He who will accomplish by His return the victory begun by His resurrection and continued in His present reign. It is He who will transform the hidden battles waged by us for Him into the day of glory which is His alone. It is He who will reveal, under the weary, humiliated features of the militant Church, the radiant countenance of the Jerusalem which descends from on high. The Church knows that this is so. No task, no trial wearies the faithful Bride. Yet none of her motherly joys can make her forget that the Bridegroom tarries still. And "The Spirit and the Bride say, Come." These are the Bible's last words.

We shall read the Bible with the Church only if we fulfill the Bible as the Church does. To read the Bible, we must live out its promise by our own expectation: living members of the living Church, we must give witness and suffer and pray; we must work for the growth of the Mystical Body which is what moves it ever forward, ever higher, towards "mature manhood, to the measure of the stature of the fullness of Christ." Then the Bible will be the "letter of God" in us at last, and it will be written "not on tablets of stone, but in our hearts."

III.

The Bible is the Book of Christ

There are Two Testaments

THE ancient Greeks reckoned dates by numbering the Olympiads, the ancient Romans by counting the years from the founding of Rome. The French sought to initiate a new era beginning with the Revolution, and the Italian Fascists sought to do the same, starting from Mussolini's march on Rome. But in Christian or formerly Christian countries, we figure dates, on calendars as in history books, by counting the years before and after Jesus Christ. We seldom give this any thought, and yet we very easily could, for it is really an affirmation that there is a central date in the whole of history, a true middle of time.

This date happens also to be the one which marks the middle of the Bible. Every child in catechism class knows—and knows by heart—that "there are two testaments, the Old and the New." The Old Testament is sacred history "before Jesus Christ." The New Testament is Jesus Christ. It is also, in advance, everything which comes "after Jesus Christ," everything which the coming of Jesus Christ means for the future of Christians and the future of the Church. The Letter to the Hebrews sets forth this basic division both in the Bible and in history: "In many and various ways God spoke of old to our fathers by the prophets;" —the whole of the Old Testament—, "but in these last days he has spoken to us by a Son," —the whole of the New.

Jesus Christ whom Both Testaments Concern

But then someone will say: What interest can we, who come after Christ and are Christians, possibly have in a provisional Old Testament, since the New Testament is here? What need have we of all those prophets, when we can hear Our Lord's own words? —And there are many Christians indeed, fervent ones too, who are content to read the Gospels, and occasionally St. Paul, without ever opening the Old Testament—except for the Psalms they find at vespers. Should they open it by chance, they are disappointed and even somewhat shocked: where is Christ in it all? Back to the Gospels and their brilliant light, they say; or else show us the Old Testament texts which clearly foretell Jesus. What do the rest matter to us?

Such talk stems from a mistaken view of the Gospel's clarity, which is the clarity of a deep pool, whose mysterious nature can be endlessly searched. It was the easiest thing in the world to meet Jesus, even to touch Him, along the roads of Galilee. But His apostles themselves, after three years of living together with Him, were still asking anxious questions about Him: "Who is this man?" — "Lord, we do not know where you are going." And Jesus sorrowfully reproaches them: "Have I been with you so long, and yet you do not know me, Philip?" At the center of our faith there is the *mystery* of Jesus. The two Testaments combine to bring this mystery before our eyes in all its truth. "Jesus Christ," says Pascal, "whom both Testaments concern: as the expectation of the Old, as the model of the New, and as the center of both."

Jesus Fulfills the Scriptures

The mystery of Jesus is the mystery of God. For Jesus comes from far away, from the outer bounds of history: "Before Abraham was, I am." He who "dwells among us" is the Word of God, and His name is the name which God told to Moses: "I am." A great deal was needed before we could measure the vastness of this presence, before the staggering fact of the Incarnation could be presented in all its truth to the scandal or to the faith of men. Sinai was needed, and the curses against Baals, and the vision of Isaiah; the progressive revelation of the absolute transcendence of God had to arouse among the Poor Ones of Israel both passionate desire and reverent fear for something so impossible: the sight of His face. It is we who must now follow still further in their footsteps, if we are to know how to look upon Jesus. To know how to sing to Christ the "Holy, holy, holy" of the Mass, we must have learned from the Old Testament the adoration of the thrice-holy God.

The mystery of Jesus is the mystery of God made man. If Jesus is "the Son of man," it is because He is the son of Abraham, the son of David. The Old Testament provides us with the long list of the Saviour's earthly ancestors, the kings and the paupers, the sinners and the just, and it tells us their glorious or tragic history, the history of the coarse and carnal people who were the chosen people, from whom Jesus was born through the Virgin Mary. Not one of these incidents is superfluous to the eventual birth of the Messiah; none of the kings of Judah should be missing from the upper galleries of our cathedrals, so that we might know that He was born of a line of men, so that we might realize how seriously we should take the prophecy: "*To us* a child is born," so that we might sing on Christmas night, in the Gospel of St. Matthew, the genealogy which plunges the Word of God into the depths of our flesh.

The mystery of Jesus is the mystery of Salvation. Just as Jesus, Word of God made flesh, sums up in Himself God's revelation to the patriarchs and the prophets, so is Jesus, the Son of man, the issue of the carnal history of the people of Israel, and so does Jesus, the Saviour of the world, at last fulfill in the work of His redeeming cross what God had conceived, begun, and foretold from the very beginning of sacred history. For the Old Testament is the history of the long and patient efforts of God to save man. And it is also the story of man's long and unruly apprenticeship in salvation. Salvation begins in a context of strength and has a carnal orientation. It moves forward through trials, and acquires an orientation which makes us understand at last what the prophets meant when they said that salvation entailed "the Law in men's hearts" and the coming of the "Servant of Yahweh" who would be rejected and humiliated, "like a lamb that is led to the slaughter," who "bore the sin of many." The Red Sea, the oppression, the deportation, Egypt and Babylon: all of these were required for the second Passover to fulfill the first—for us to sing to Christ the *Exultet* of the paschal vigil and the "Lamb of God" of the communion service.

"Search the Scriptures," Jesus said, "they bear witness to me." We search the Scriptures—all the Scriptures—if we want to know and to acknowledge Christ.

IV.

The Bible is the Book
of the Church

The Bible and the Christian

THERE are Christians who go to Church regularly and yet, once
they have returned home, never open the Bible; they are making
a mistake. Then there are others who read the Bible, and begin
to think they have nothing more to learn from their pastor; they
are making a still greater mistake. The Bible, quite simply, is
not left to the curiosity or even the devotion of an individual, but
has been given to the whole Church. To read it well, we need
the help of the whole Church.

—But is it not true that God spoke directly to men, and cannot we too place ourselves, through the Bible, in the presence
of God, so as to listen to Him without any intermediary? And
does not the *Imitation* write: "Let not Moses speak unto me,
nor any of the prophets, but rather do thou speak, O Lord
God, ... for thy servant heareth."

—All this is surely true. As we have said, the Bible is the
Word of God spoken to each one of us. It is also, for each one
of us, the book of prayer, of secret and personal prayer as well as
of public and collective prayer. But even then, even when we
are alone with our Bible, the Church is with us, reading it and
necessarily guiding us.

The Word of God Creates the People of God

In the Old Testament, no one came closer to God than did Moses, with whom God spoke "as a man speaks to his friend." In the New Testament, no one came closer to God than did St. Paul, who was caught up to the third heaven and heard "things that cannot be told, which man may not utter." Now God made Himself known to Moses only so that He could send him to his brethren, and put upon his shoulders the burden of His people. And on the road to Damascus, when Paul asked, "Who are you, Lord?", he received in answer: "I am Jesus, whom you are persecuting." Paul had never known Jesus and was persecuting only the Christians: the Christ who spoke to him must then be one with His people. This was how Paul understood it. From then on, "the care of all the churches" never left him. The Word of God was addressed neither to Moses nor to Paul for themselves or because of themselves; it was spoken to them for the People of God.

We must therefore draw our conclusion: God did not come to save several "noble souls," He came to save "His people." And the Bible is not something intended for the personal satisfaction of us "initiates," it is the constitution of that people. The Israel, first, with whom the Covenant was made. And then Israel enlarged into the people of the New Covenant, "Israel according to the Spirit"—the Church. The parables are filled with comparisons which suggest this: a kingdom, a net filled with fish, a harvest, a wedding banquet—the image is always one of a gathering together. The Twelve are called to go preach to "all nations"; Simon receives the name Peter, for "on this rock I will build my church." The Eucharist is a common meal, and the blood of Calvary is shed "for many." Finally, at Pentecost, the

Holy Spirit makes the apostles speak in all languages to announce the resurrection. And we, in our turn, built as we are "upon the foundation of the apostles and prophets, Christ Jesus himself being the chief cornerstone," are no longer straying children or scattered rubble, but a Church, a solid and cohesive spiritual edifice in which the affirmation of the same faith and the mutual service of charity makes of us all a single temple of God.

God wills the Church to be. The Word of God creates the Church. If we listen to this Word, though we be in the silence of a monk's cell, it brings us all together. It brings back to our minds again and again that only the community matters. It brings us a call which goes beyond our powers, a call which only a people can hear.

The Church Opens the Bible for Us

Why should we be surprised, then, if we cannot understand the Bible by ourselves? The Church has preserved the Bible from generation to generation. She has kept it intact, adding nothing and taking nothing away. And it is to the Church that the understanding of the Bible has been entrusted. The Church is, in the words of the First Vatican Council, "the guardian and the teacher of the Word of God." She is its guardian, not for the purpose of concealing it, but so as to be able to offer it complete and pure to all her children. She is its teacher, not for the purpose of passing judgment on it, but so as to be able to listen to it and to repeat it. Each one of us is too limited to live the history of the People of God all by himself, and to understand on his own the Bible, which is the history of that people. But the Church is familiar with her own history. Like Our Lady, she "ponders all these things in her heart." She alone has a heart great enough for this Word, for she was made by this Word. She alone has a heart faithful enough, for she is protected by God.

It follows that we must live with the Church if the Word is to become for us the bread which she will break with us as she breaks the Eucharistic bread. And it is with her that we must read the Bible. With the Church—with her hierarchy, the pope and the bishops, who have the authority to explain it to us, since they are the successors of those to whom Christ said, "Who hears you, hears me." With the Church—with the Fathers and theologians who have meditated on the Bible throughout the centuries: it is not too much to expect that this uninterrupted collective effort will support our own and help us to contemplate its mysteries. With the Church—with her liturgy: ever since the Church began to pray, she has used the whole Bible in her prayer; by praying with her, the whole Bible gradually becomes familiar to us. With the Church—with all the saints who have read the Bible on their knees, with all of our brethren who have sought and found light in the Bible and who pass it down to us so that we can make the same discovery for ourselves. With the Church—with your catechism, which condenses the revelation of the Bible to aid your memory, and which will guide your reflections anew when you go back to the Bible yourself. With the Church—with your parish: your pastor's sermon, the solemn Mass on Sunday, the charity from day to day. For the parish is in the Church, and where the Church is, there too is the Spirit. And where the Spirit is, the Spirit "who spoke through the prophets," there we can read the Bible: read it as it was written, in the Spirit of Truth.

V.

The Bible is a Mirror

"Close-Ups" and Pocket Mirrors . . .

We have all seen at the movies what is called a "close-up": at some dramatic moment, the screen shows only the face of the star, enlarged so as to fill the screen completely. If the director, the cameraman, and the star have all done their work well, what we see is no longer the suddenly gigantic details of a face but, through them, the emotion which is being expressed. We have the impression of penetrating straight to the heart with a single glance.

Each of us from time to time also looks with interest on the "close-up" of himself. The gentleman who assumes an energetic air in front of his mirror after shaving, the young girl who wonders, as she looks in the mirror, if her fiancé will find her pretty today, see nothing in the hundred square inches of polished glass but their own image. And, not without a certain satisfaction, they recognize themselves: "Me."

Indeed! Is it really you? Isn't the little mirror just as deceiving as the "close-up" at the movies? When Julie Christie leaves the studio where a clever cameraman captured on film all the distress of the poor abandoned girl she plays, she ceases "being" the poor girl in about three seconds, gets into her Cadillac, and goes off to her favorite haunts (about which *Photoplay* and *Modern Screen* give us quite complete information). No, it is not Julie Christie whom we saw. But do we see ourselves any better in our bathroom mirror? We too are caught up again by life, which rips our mask away and gives us a completely different image, one made up of our actions, our generous deeds, our egoisms, an image whose reflection sometimes surprises us in the look of those whose paths we cross during life.

But is even this image a faithful one? Do others—those who see us, those who love us—know us better than we know ourselves? We know quite well that they are mistaken, that there is something in us which eludes them, for better or for worse, and which even eludes us. We are neither our faces nor our actions, but our hearts. And what mirror will show a man his heart?

The Sword and the Mirror

But this is the kind of mirror that the Bible offers to every one of us. For this mirror reflects neither our own gaze nor the gaze of other men but the gaze of God. God alone knows man, God alone knows each individual man. The Bible, by revealing God to us, brings us face to face with the gaze which sees us as we are. Along with the mystery of God and His love for us, the Bible gradually provides us with glimpses, throughout the course of sacred history, of the secret of the beings we are, the beings God has loved.

What, then, is the secret? It can be summed up in a few words: Man was created in God's image, was deformed by sin, was formed again in the image of Christ. This is our true face, and no human gaze has ever succeeded in plumbing its triple depth. For "all men are liars," sometimes heeding the false prom-

71

ise: "You will be like God," and sometimes the counsels of despair: "Eat, drink, and be merry, for tomorrow we die." Man knows neither his true greatness nor his true misery. It is creative and redeeming love who "knows what is in man" and uncovers it for us by His self-revelation to us. The "old man" and the "new man"; the splendor of the creature, the horror of sin, and the untasted freshness of the "Saviour's springs" within us; only before God, under His gaze, and in His Word, do we discover, little by little, the reality of life, death, and resurrection.

This is why the Bible is the mirror held up before each one of us, as St. James says, in which a man can observe "the face he was born with"—and the face with which he was reborn (Jas. 1, 23–25). But he will not see it, or having seen it will at once "forget" what it was like, unless he seek first in faith for the gaze of Him who "discerns the thoughts and intentions of the heart," unless he recognize his own misery and at last cries out: "Lord, what will you have me do?" For, as St. Paul says, the Bible is also "sharper than any two-edged sword," to be carried throughout our lives, the scalpel "piercing to the division of soul and spirit, of joints and marrow, and discerning the thoughts and intentions of the heart" (Heb. 4, 12).

Veronica's Veil

"The thoughts and intentions of the heart" are thus "discerned," all through the Bible, by the Word of God: thoughts and intentions of men whose story the Bible tells us, David or Job, Pilate or Nicodemus, Peter or Judas—and ours as well as theirs. Face to face with the call of God, these men discover what they are, and they uncover for us something of the image of man which we are seeking and which, disfigured and dimmed, we bear within ourselves. But where are we to find the image without spot or wrinkle, the real "face we are born with," the man "according to God's heart"?

He is here. "Behold the man," the man in whom are summed up all creation, all sin, all grace. For He is the Son of God and He is in our flesh: born of the Virgin Mary, weary beside the well at Sychar, talking with us, transfigured on Tabor, going up to Jerusalem for the triumph on the Cross, covered with sweat during the agony at Gethsemane, dying on the tree, erect on Easter morning. He is "the most beautiful of the children of men," "the man of sorrows," the crucified "made sin" for us, the conqueror who "lives unto God."

His face is "the image of the invisible God," but it is also *our* image—the image of our vocation. There is only one thing which God wishes of us, and it is, as St. Paul says, that we "be conformed to the image of his Son." God's gaze on us passes through Jesus and illumines for us the image of Jesus. The Bible is a mirror because, like Veronica's Veil, it preserves this image for us. The Bible is a mirror because it is the truest and the greatest "Book of the Imitation of Jesus Christ." The Bible is a mirror because it reflects the gaze of Jesus for us—the same gaze which called the rich young man to perfection: "And Jesus looking upon him loved him"; and the gaze which converted the sinner: "And the Lord turned and looked at Peter." . . .

When we read the Bible, we find that we see in it our own features mingled with those of Jesus. This was how Francis of Assisi read it, and was transformed into the *Poverello* by hearing a single Gospel read in church—"Take neither money nor staff nor a change of tunic." This was how Père de Foucauld read it, lovingly conforming his life to the life at Nazareth. But it is also the way the Church reads it for us, faithfully putting before our eyes on every occasion—nuptial Masses and funeral Masses, Christmas vigils and paschal vigils—"the face that we were born with"—that we might be born anew.

VI.

The Bible
is the Book of Prayer

The Ways of Prayer

When Moses, at the Burning Bush, heard the call of God for the
first time, he took the sandals from his feet and fell down with
his face to the earth. When the mission to deliver his people was
given to him, he vehemently protested of his unworthiness: "Who
am I that I should . . . bring the sons of Israel out of Egypt?"
Later he became bold enough to ask God to tell him "His name,"
really to tell him something about His nature and his glory.

Moses had many more meetings with God. We see him "crying
to the Lord" to save his brothers from the swords of the Egyp-
tians, from hunger and thirst in the desert, to pardon their
murmuring and their apostasy. We see him joyously taking up
the song of his sister Miriam after the passage through the Red
Sea: "I will sing to the Lord, for he has triumphed gloriously."
We see him climbing alone to the summit of Sinai, patiently
listening to everything God says to him. We see him speaking
with God in the Tent "as a man speaks to his friend." And we
see him making anew the impossible request: "Show me thy
glory."

All of this is prayer. Although far too many Christians think so, prayer is not merely a request made to God or to His saints to obtain help and protection at serious moments in life, much less to draw a winning number in the Irish Sweepstakes or be accepted by a college. Prayer is something great and mysterious, as God and man are, and, in prayer, God and man meet. When one resolves to seek God, he must give the whole of himself, and his search will never end. This is why prayer has so many roads, all of which lead to God and no one of which is sufficient. Rather than being satisfied with one road, we must, like Moses himself, take each in its turn. We must take the road of adoration and of wonder—for God is great. We must take the road of humility and of repentance—for God is holy and we are sinners. We must take the road of petition—for God is strength while we are weakness, God is wealth and we abjection. We must take the road of praise and of thanksgiving—for God is good and His creatures are good. We must take the road of friendship—for it is God who comes to us. We must take the road of contemplation and of silence—for God is perfect Truth and perfect Beauty and we are made to lose ourselves in Him.

Lord, Teach Us to Pray

But do we know *how* to pray? Prayer, according to the catechism —and we now see what it means—, is a "raising of the mind and heart to God." Can it really be God we are thinking about, when we know Him so little? Can it really be God we are praying to? Is it really our "mind and heart" which are being raised to Him —our "mind and heart" is our whole life, with all the ardor of our loves, all the weight of our sins, with our neighbor for whom we are responsible? Prayer implies that a man is praying and

76

that God is being prayed to—but man, so prone to distraction, hardly knows God at all. It is easy to understand why the apostles asked Jesus one day, after they had seen Him pray: *"Lord, teach us to pray."*

Now we see why the Bible is our book of prayer. The Bible gives us both the revelation of God and the knowledge of ourselves, and does this so well that the spark of prayer can be struck. The Bible reveals God because it is the Word of God, manifested to us, and because it is the book of Christ, "God with us." The Bible reveals us to ourselves because it is a mirror, in which we discover what we are, what we can be, what God expects of us. The well-springs of prayer are opened to the man who reads the Bible with faith and sincerity, and the time will come when he can read it only on his knees. For the Bible will have become the place where he meets God. Like Moses, he can only throw himself face-down, offering up a prayer of wonder or of fear, repentance or bold confidence, insistent petition or jubilant thanksgiving. The roads of prayer are no longer unknown roads for him, for the Word of God has cleared them all.

Praying with the Bible

Not only have they been cleared before us, but we are no longer all alone. Others have followed them before: all the men we meet in sacred history, saints and sinners, men of action and men of silence, kings and paupers, and all of them men of prayer. We need but follow in their footsteps, make their words, their songs, their cries our own. No longer are we solitary pilgrims. On all the roads of prayer, there are crowds who have gone before. A seemingly endless procession, rather, raising their voices in song and waiting only for us to fall into step and lend our voices.

In doing this, we can follow our own mood, respond according to our own needs, in song or in silence. We can pray in hushed voices, like the prophetess Anna before the Ark of the Covenant; we can pray with eyes filled with tears, like Peter or Mary Magdalene; we can argue with God, as Job did; we can sing like Miriam, we can even dance like David or leap high in the air like the cripple cured by Jesus. And our prayer, in being joined to theirs, becomes all the greater and is the prayer of the people of God, strong with the faith and hope and love of all our brothers of both Testaments, strong with the Spirit who drives them onward and prays with them.

This is why the Church's public and liturgical prayer puts incessantly on our lips the words of the Bible. The Church has meditated on the Bible for so long that she no longer finds other words in which to pray. She knows that Our Lady's song of the *Magnificat* came from the Canticle of Anna and from words of the Psalms which sprang spontaneously to her lips from their place within her heart. She knows that Our Lord prayed with the Bible, and that His last cry from the Cross was a verse from the Psalms. She herself leads her children along the very roads she has never ceased to follow. With Job she prays for her dead, with Tobit and Sarah she prays for young couples, at Mass she recalls the sacrifices of Abraham and of Melchizedek. The new People of God takes up the *Amen* which resounds no longer in an ancient temple built by men. In hailing with its alleluia the resurrection of Christ, our passover, it echoes the liturgical acclamation which was even then a part of the imperfect and provisional passover. And the rosary, too, prayer of great public petition and prayer of the distraught who has lost his power of words, the rosary simply repeats unwearyingly the two most beautiful prayers in the Bible.

THIRD PART

THE LETTER AND THE SPIRIT

Some Notes for Further Reflection

I.

Biblical Questions and the Life of the Church Today

THE Word of God, whose written witness is the Bible, is addressed to the Church for her own nourishment and for communication by her to the world. In this double sense the Bible belongs to the Church. Though biblical questions will ever call for expert scholarship, they can never be merely biblical questions, for they are bound up with the life of the Church. Changed conditions within the Church's life can, moreover, produce modifications in the posture of biblical questions. We are here devoting our attention to the "biblical crossroads" we have reached today, but we are quite well aware that our contribution is in the nature of a cursory glance. We gladly offer it to those whose competence exceeds our own, and hope that it will stimulate constructive criticism and clarification.

We propose to study the new posture of biblical questions from two points of view: the Bible as the witness the Church must offer to the *world;* the Bible as the food of the Church's *own* life.

1. BIBLICAL QUESTIONS AND THE CRISIS IN CULTURE

Although the sacred books were originally the exclusive preserve of the faithful, this is no longer the case. Today, any passer-by can enter church during Mass. And the common reader, no matter what his dispositions, can open the sacred text, which has simply become one of the elements in the Church's image, one of the faces she offers to the world, whether to scandalize or to convert. The sacred books are, in consequence, one of the disputed areas where Church and world find themselves in contact: they are either the nerve-center of disbelief's frontal attack or the point through which Christian faith penetrates human culture. Hence it is of no small importance for the Church, in her apostolic mission, to be aware of the desires and demands which motivate men outside the Church in their encounter with her in this area, and to see what "biblical questions" are actually presented to her.

We must take account of the fact that these desires and demands are in process of a profound transformation. Talk of a crisis in culture is a commonplace. But what is its impact on biblical questions?

In the past, non-committed intellectuals usually approached the Bible in "historical" terms and summoned Catholics, like it or not, before the bar of history. (Someone has spoken of the "tyranny" of history over the modern world.) "It was up to us historians," wrote Henri Davenson in 1939, "to say whether belief in God was necessary, whether *The Iliad* was a work of art, whether Bohemia was a nation. . . ." History, as elevated by Renan to the status of an "exact science of the things of the spirit," seemed certain of its principles and methods. Its principles were derived from positivist science rather than from metaphysics, and its methods were those of the laboratory, transposed to another realm.

An honest demand for truth, but with criteria limited by that truth, history was thus applied to the study of the Bible. Since Christianity made an explicit claim to be linked to a particular history, its scientific credentials had to be examined. The first step in the process was to get rid of the *a priori* hypothesis—contrary, in any event, to the scientist's metaphysics—which dogmatic faith represented. There is no need to go through once again the story of the intense conflict between faith and reason on the subject of Christian beginnings.

The reaction which took place in the Church is a familiar story. Although the reflexes of fear were undoubtedly in evidence, the "counsels of prudence" were also on hand. There were a few who just gave up the battle and, despairing of preserving biblical dogma intact against the critical onslaught, no longer claimed for it any status as historical truth. Earlier, they had similarly rejected the metaphysical proofs for the existence of God, who "is no more a character in history" as Loisy said, "than he is an element in the physical world." God and God's Word were to be sought by other methods, less "profane," the methods of religious experience, individual or collective. In this way, faith would have to account only to itself, while facts, even "dogmatic facts," would be left to the field of criticism.[1]

But in spite of such deficiencies and errors, the Church did not

[1] To this Modernist view corresponds the Barthian conception, which differs from it in affirming the absolute transcendence of God, and yet is similar to it in removing from history's objectivity the temporal relationship of the believer with his God.

remain without an answer to the questions posed by history. The intellectual courage of a Père Lagrange, among others, lay in accepting historical methodology, with no reservation other than that of honest scholarship, and in believing firmly enough in the Word of God to be convinced that the Bible, when better understood in its human structure, could only bear more perfectly the message awaited by faith. There can no longer be any question of the value of the results achieved by the immense historical and exegetical effort undertaken by a few generous groups on behalf of the whole Church. For even though the majority of "critical" positions received their formulation or limits at that time, as a result of new discoveries or simply through developments in research, the theology of inspiration, once it was better understood, would make it possible for Catholics to acknowledge with confidence the human conditioning of the Word of God. Historical method could then, in freedom and in certainty, give greater definition to the insertion in time of the interventions of the Christian "God of dates and places." During the same period, Père Gardeil, in his analysis of the act of faith, was demonstrating both its legitimacy vis-à-vis reason (the "motives for credibility") and its transcendent freedom, in obedience to the word of God alone, vis-à-vis any rational motivation.

This is all part of our present intellectual equipment. Still in all, we have to admit that the concerns of the cultivated are no longer the same as those which occupied the attention of a Père Lagrange. And yet it would be a mistake to think that this great era of biblical studies, roughly bounded by the encyclicals *Providentissimus Deus* of Leo XIII (1893) and *Divino Afflante Spiritu* of Pius XII (1943), has achieved all that it could and that we can now move on to other things. No doubt, the "biblical question," in the form in which it was presented during the Modernist period, has completely lost its former poignancy for the intellectuals, whose curiosity and concern have taken another direction. Categories of thought, though, even when replaced by others in the vital sector of a given culture, can nonetheless retain their importance in the broader and humbler sectors in which that culture survives under more or less degraded forms. In our own times, this is very likely true of the categories—and prejudices—of historical criticism. A radically outdated book like Renan's *Life of Jesus,* for example, probably still awakens in a number of minds the very doubts and questions which the experts have long since disposed of. Now this extended life, among all those nourished on a received culture, of questions previously debated by the giants of thought is not lacking in significance for cultural development. It does, in any event, directly affect the life of a Church which has the mission of evangelizing the poor. This pastoral consideration makes it impossible for us to quit—indeed, it requires us to make more generally accessible—the field in which Père Lagrange and his rivals operated.

Most important of all—no matter what the present state of affairs might be—, this field is fruitful *in itself,* and essential to the faith of the Church. At the very heart of the catholic Creed, the historical entry of God into time: "under Pontius Pilate," is affirmed, in the affirmation of the Incarnation. The faith of the Church is bound up with historical, contingent facts: "If Christ has not been raised, our faith is in vain" (1 Cor. 15, 14). The historical method which allows us to have a firmer grasp on facts like these is a permanent contribution to theology. The life of the Church is in this way enriched by something which had originally been a necessary measure of defense.

It is nonetheless true that profound changes have occurred on the cultural scene. Although the Bible must, of course, remain a favored point of contact between Church and world, the fact is that biblical *criticism* is no longer the precise area in which the Church encounters the world's concerns—the most vital concerns, at any rate. This can be shown by a consideration of the new directions taken by culture, as indicative of a new feeling about the Bible—on the part of the cultivated man, and also on the part of the man in the street.

We will here summarize the "historian's sadness" which was so masterfully analyzed by Davenson shortly before World War II.

History as the "exact science of the things of the spirit" (Renan) has gone into bankruptcy. The efforts of generations of historians have not led to a "science of history," valid for all, but to "a series of different viewpoints on history." Each new synthesis destroys the one which preceded it, so that nothing of it remains, and each new synthesis awaits its replacement by the next. And, quite apart from any effort at synthesis, not even the simplest *facts* escape the drive towards "objectivity"—since "the well-attested material fact is, in the final analysis, less likely to be 'certain,' to be raised to the famous category of 'knowledge valid for all,' than the fact that no one has yet deemed it worthwhile to dispute it."

Why this failure? And what are we to learn from it? In our desire to impose on historical knowledge the impossible ideal of "exact science," we have failed to see what constitutes its originality: its *human* object. We cannot lay hold of "equivocal and inexhaustible" human reality by extrapolating the univocal processes of the laboratory. The mystery of human activity does not disappear simply because that activity is past. Moreover, the past, scientifically known, does not make it possible to foresee the future. It is, in fact, only the man who has a future and who shapes his own destiny, only the "committed" historian, who can understand the human past, in a way which is somehow analogous to the act of faith. History, rejecting an impossible "objectivity," must strive to be "personalist."

We can now see the point of departure and the point of destination of this evolution. The positivist ideal of history was fashioned on the model of science. In order to restore value to history, what is now called for is a metaphysics—whose primary place in the things of the spirit has once again been asserted, as it was in the past. But not any kind of metaphysics. The metaphysics which will make the historian capable of integrating "equivocal and inexhaustible" human reality with the past can only be a metaphysics in which *man* finds his proper place, a place marked not only by a "nature" but also by the possibility of a *destiny*. Metaphysics can make history possible only if it is a metaphysics of historical man.

The crisis of history, then, is in the final analysis just a special chapter in the *philosophical* crisis of culture, what Jean Wahl has called the "struggle to the death between abstract thought and existence" which has been waged since the time of Hegel and Kierkegaard. We have no intention of intering into that discussion here, but content ourselves with pointing out, in aid of our object, certain salient themes of Kierkegaardian thought, themes which are undoubtedly suggestive of several underlying tendencies in the over-all movement of contemporary philosophy.

The first is the rejection of "system." For when we conceive of man on the basis of his place in the order of natures, when we conceive of his activities as moments in an abstract dialectic, we fail to see his proper *existence,* an existence which is expressed in passion and in choice. Man can then be defined as freedom. And it is his history rather than his nature which makes us know him. Man can be enriched and determined, therefore, not by a particular objective contribution of revelation or civilization, or by the development of a dialectic in which he is caught up, but by the paradox of an *event* in which his own freedom encounters another, a transcendent freedom.

This rejection of system leads us to conceive of truth not as the "objective" and inevitable result of a dialectic which cannot be eluded, but as the term of man's most subjective activity. *"An objective uncertainty held fast in an appropriation-process of the most passionate inwardness is the truth,* the highest truth attainable for an *existing* individual." And Kierkegaard continues: "But the above definition of truth is an equivalent expression for faith."[2]

In sum, the expression of truth is unabashedly indirect. Truth thus "interiorized" cannot be the object of systematic exposition. Hence, in Kierkegaard himself, the play of pseudonyms and the dramatization of spheres of existence—simply the transcription of the philosophical drama which made up his own life. Existence itself—or imaginary existence—is the adequate mode of expression in philosophy.

Categories of thought like these have an intrinsic orientation towards an encounter with the Bible—so much more surely in that they stemmed largely from Kierkegaard's own meditation, as a Christian, on the Bible. There is a history in which God intervenes in a paradoxical way; this history is again con-

[2] *Concluding Unscientific Postscript,* Princeton, 1941, p. 182.

temporary with faith, and with faith alone; revelation is incarnation—this is the actual content and inspiration of Kierkegaardian dialectic.

It is evident that contemporary thought remains largely unaffected by this biblical content. But may we not, and in modes of thought which are most remote from the Bible, find themes which approach those which in Kierkegaard were biblical themes? Both Marxist Hegelianism and contemporary existentialism are less interested in man's nature than in his historic destiny. For them, too, truth has ceased to be objective and has joined hands with existence. For them, too, the philosopher's task is less to expose truth than to make truth incarnate by action. What is more, we find these very themes in the nonphilosopher, to the extent that he, as a Marxist, has become aware of his membership in a class which has a destiny in history, or, as one enslaved, has discovered that man is truly man only in his freedom. All of this, however far removed it may be from the Bible which inspired Kierkegaard, has nevertheless helped to bring about a certain awareness on the part of today's man— something quite different from what existed in the past—which, once the Bible is known, can quite readily be harmonized with it.

One of the tasks of the Church today is to make the Bible known in such a way that it will have an effect on this new awareness.

It is not that this awareness must be accepted purely and simply as the criterion of what is true, for it is a mixture of error and truth. And the day must certainly come when existentialism is brought to trial, when the defense of the "object"—in the very name of "existence"—is undertaken. However that may be, a Catholic presentation of the biblical message can certainly not forsake its objective truth, either as to natures and their order, in creation, under the domain of sin and under the domain of grace, or as to facts. "If Christ *has* not been raised," there is precious little significance in the passionate affirmation I might employ to make the illusion of His resurrection my own. Viewed from this angle, the heritage of the work and the spirit of the critical era, as well as the heritage of speculative theology's great achievements, must not be cast aside.

But if the Church owes *this* generation not only the correction of its errors but also an answer to its authentic aspirations, may we not think that the Church's tremendous biblical tradition bears such an answer within itself? To the "historical" man, indifferent to systems and suspicious of objective knowledge, the Church can recall that her revelation is, before all else, a history: the history of God's free interventions, the history of men called by God; that this history becomes our own past only by becoming our present; that its truth is attained in its "equivocal and inexhaustible reality"—in the mystery of God—only by faith; that this history is lived from now on by "witnesses who go to the slaughter." What is, in short, asked of the Church is that biblical history regain its position as "sacred history." The humble texture of facts, in their literal terms—but also their mysterious import in the dialectic of the two Testaments; critical attention to language and to forms, to dates and to places— but also faith as unifying light and organizing principle; the honesty of the historian—but also the life of the Church engaged in the history which she recounts . . . Such a presentation of the Bible, in a fully Christian light, can undoubtedly be accepted only by faith, but it would undoubtedly be better *listened to* by most men today than the simple introductions of apologetics are.

What is thus proposed to the Church as a "new" demand made by men in the world amounts really to a simple proposal that the Church *appropriate* the Bible for herself as her *own* history. Actually, the demand is an ancient one which the Church must impose upon herself in every era. It so happens that certain contemporary developments in her life have made this demand still more urgent. We must now take account of them.

2. THE BIBLICAL MOVEMENT

The Bible has never been forgotten in the Church. It could not be, without the Church's very essence being affected, since everything in the Church—dogma, morality, sacraments, prayer, ecclesiastical formation—is nourished by biblical revelation. And yet it is true that certain Christian ages have lived more generally and more fully on the Bible. The age of the Fathers and even, in many respects, the great medieval centuries strike us as periods when language, forms of thought, spirituality, imagination were scriptural. Psalms were sung by the congregation, biblical readings in the liturgy were understandable to all, preaching was in homilies, theology was reflection on the sacred text. Inasmuch as a specifically Christian culture existed, it was a biblical culture.

It cannot be questioned that the last years of the 19th century and the early years of the 20th—whose habits of mind are far from having disappeared—, when contrasted with the great periods of biblical culture, offer a distressing picture. To be sure, the Bible was always present in the Breviary, in the Missal, in theological arguments. But must we not admit that this indispensable presence was frequently reduced to the bare minimum? Life had to be sustained from that source, yet the "pilgrimage to the sources" was seldom undertaken. The trip was recognized as a dangerous one, and it was left to the bold. Moreover, the prevailing rationalism, with which many Christians were unconsciously imbued, predisposed them to confusion in the face of the unpredictable and occasionally shocking freedom of divine actions and expressions, as abundantly set forth in the Bible. Consequently, no one moved from the base of Sinai, quite content to believe, to hope, to pray, to merit, and above all to think at secondhand. One of the most distressing things about the situation was that Christianity began to be a bore.[3]

This situation could not last. For reasons proper to the Church —and, at the root of them, the action of the Holy Spirit which sets it in motion—, and for general reasons—the development of culture, a biblical movement in the Church was born. We shall try to sketch the currents within that movement, so as to deduce from them the tasks which fall to biblical exegesis.

A primary current stemmed from the liturgical movement. We do not intend to seek its causes in detail. As a matter of fact, the causes of a liturgical movement—or a biblical movement, or a missionary movement—are always present in the Church, and there is no need to look for them elsewhere. It does seem, though, that they were stimulated at that time because of the very crisis

[3] Of course, all this is true only: (1) with many striking exceptions. Consider the biblical freshness, kept alive by daily contact with the very letter of the Gospels, of the spirituality of a St. Thérèse of Lisieux or a Charles de Foucauld; (2) while reserving final judgment. Deficiencies in the explicit *awareness* with which the Church recognizes the Bible as her own history do not warrant concluding to a *real* infidelity by the Church to this history, or throwing doubt on the authentically biblical value of her faith and works.

in culture which we have already described under other aspects. Because of the rationalist emaciation of what has been called by Jean Rostand "the ice age of the human spirit," a return to man in his full reality, spiritual and carnal, tangible and communal, was indicated.[4] The conditions for a liturgical movement were thereupon present, however little attention might have been given to the sacramental actions of Christian worship. But, by the same token, the conditions, and the necessity, for a biblical movement were present as well.

To begin with, the liturgy is made up of readings which are for the most part biblical readings. As soon as the means are found to make them listened to, or to make them understandable to the faithful, these readings reacquire their traditional role as an introduction to the letter of the sacred text. To this first and by no means unimportant benefit of the liturgical movement, a second is immediately added: the introduction afforded by the liturgy is far more than the simple material knowledge of the Bible, and is actually an inimitably artful introduction to the spiritual understanding of the Bible. The choices, relationships, allusions, even the contradictions present in the liturgy bring about the development of an incomparable biblical sensitivity in everyone who surrenders himself to it. Last of all, and most importantly, the liturgy in its deepest sense, centered as it is on the Mass, is the incorporation and active participation of the faithful in the salvation-event. If the Bible is the history of this event, the liturgy is the affirmation, each day renewed, that this history is our own. When thus seen as spiritual understanding of the Bible and as positive integration of all of sacred history

---

[4] See Romano Guradini's beautiful book, *The Spirit of the Liturgy*, New York, 1935.

into the living Church, it is immediately clear how the liturgical movement activates the biblical movement which is born of it.

Another current in the biblical movement stems from "Catholic ecumenism"—the renewed attention, prayer, and work for the reunion of the Church. This current undoubtedly affects smaller groups than the preceding currents, and yet it touches on essential aspects of the Church's life and of her bonds with the Bible. Faced with the reality of separation, we discovered that separation would not be overcome by any concessions, but only by loyal and mutual understanding and by a common effort to accept fully the message of Christ to which it bears witness. For a Catholic, this means both a new understanding of the catholicity, the totality of the Church of Rome, a catholicity capable of accepting every partial truth, and the refusal to leave any element of this catholicity "under the bushel basket." This demands, in the first place, the willingness to restore to full appreciation the elements of the Church which form the deepest sources of her life and which antedate, both in their nature and in their history, the division. And thus, again: the Fathers, the liturgy, the Scriptures.

Some purpose might be served by emphasizing the common components of the different currents in the biblical movement in the Church and by pointing out, in conclusion, the tasks which fall on specialists in biblical questions as well as on all those who bear any responsibility for Christian teaching or culture. These tasks flow spontaneously from the needs of non-Christian thought as well as from the needs of the Church herself.

The notion of *sacred history* must be rediscovered and exploited. (The sense in which we mean this should be sufficiently clear from all that has already been said.) This demands especially the reclarification, for the benefit of modern man, of the relationship between the Old and the New Testament, along with an exact sense of human context and also a sense of the mystery of the preparations. It also demands a more precise presentation of biblical eschatology, so essential to the Church's integration of the biblical message.

Something else which is needed—and this task is closely connected with the preceding—is a new approach to the problem of the *meanings* of the Bible: a definition of the relationships between historical method and faith, between the literal meaning and the "spiritual meaning"; and a demonstration of how, prior to any speculative effort, the biblical facts themselves are the best possible nourishment for the religious man.

Last of all, the bond between the Bible and *the Church* must be clearly shown. We must show how the Bible lives within the Church and finds historical coherence in the Church alone. And thus we must bring new life to the old discussion about Scripture and Tradition.

These are, primarily, theological tasks. But, in the Church, theology is separated neither from preaching nor from the life of the faithful. This is why these tasks are, though on different levels, proposed to *all*. The restoration of a true biblical culture among the clergy is particularly necessary. It is also essential that the faithful, through the liturgy, through instruction, through preaching, through personal contact with the text, once again draw their life from the Bible by drawing more life from the Church. The encyclical *Divino Afflante Spiritu,* after recalling the previous fifty years' work in biblical exegesis and after setting forth the Catholic charter for biblical research, offers to all those who must derive profit from already accumulated labors and riches a number of exhortations to vigorous action, and it would be presumptuous to pretend to add to them. We are content to quote, with the encyclical, St. Jerome: "Ignorance of the Scriptures is ignorance of Christ."

II.

Literal and Religious Exegesis of the Old Testament

READING the Old Testament as Christians—if this reading is to be both honest and fruitful—must be a "literal" reading above all. It must seek, within the texts, the *literal meaning,* that is, what the author meant to say and did say.

We say that this is necessary for a *Christian* reading. It is self-evident that literal study is required of one who sees the Bible as a document in the history of religions (which it certainly is), but this is not what we have in mind. It is also self-evident if one sees the Bible as a literary treasure, a monument of our culture—something which our professors of humanities (even when they are Christians, even when they are priests) manage serenely to ignore while initiating their students into Homer and Virgil: there is a great deal that could be said on the subject, but we shall not press the point, for this is not what we have in mind either.

What we do have in mind is the search for the *Word of God* in the Old Testament. We are saying that this Word will not be heard, or will be heard badly, confusing it with other words, respectable perhaps but of different origin, unless the effort is made to pay close attention to the precise content of the texts, and unless this attention is docile to the reality of the texts themselves.

These are, it should be noted, properly *religious* considerations which prompt us to recommend the literal exegesis which is so often faulted as disrespectful of the sacred text. It seems to us that the time has come to do it justice. To be sure, profane "curiosity," erudite research, can, through literal study, lead faithful reading astray and distract it from its object. But faithful reading is no less threatened, and the respect due to the Word of God no less imperiled, by a kind of presumption from which "spiritual" exegetes are not always immune: thinking they know beforehand what the texts have to say to us and provoking them to say things they do not say, they thereby make themselves incapable of seeing *what they do say,* of hearing their special message. Out of a determination to read the Old Testament "in the light of the New," they forget the special light of the Old, which the New has fulfilled and not abolished. Consequently, they ignore, without realizing it, irreplaceable riches of the Word of God, riches which are not amenable to our syntheses.

Literal exegesis, when practiced by the believing reader and oriented towards a faithful reading, will be wary of this temptation. Literal exegesis will keep in mind, while avoiding all sophistry—including the pious kind—, a simple matter of fact: if we want to know what God wanted to say to us, it makes more sense to start by looking into what He *did say.* Literal exegesis will thus be marked by the authenticity of its approach. More positively still, literal exegesis will also be the subtle and dependable instrument through which faith will perceive—under the orchestration of the Fathers and the liturgy, even under the pure song of the Gospel—certain notes, muffled but essential, without which there would be no song, certain basic harmonics of the genuine Word of God, certain as yet unresolved cries in the Christian harmony, all of which the Christian always benefits from hearing.

This is not to say that spontaneous reading of the Old Testament does not hold for the unprepared Christian disappointments which can lead even to disgust. No doubt, this experience is common to many of those who, swept along by the "biblical movement," just opened a Bible with which they were unfamiliar. Although the New Testament might be somewhat familiar to them, their first contacts with the Old strike them with a strangeness which is difficult to overcome.

Undoubtedly, if they persevere, they will be well rewarded for their trouble by the unexpected discovery of passages which can be understood without commentary and disclose to them things not previously known and yet immediately assimilable into their theological lives: the Decalogue, in its stark brevity, cleansed of the singsong of our "commandments of God"; the promise and the faith of Abraham, potentially restorative of the concern a Christian should have lest he know but poorly "the gift of God"; the vision of Isaiah, which introduces them to the shattering experience of divine holiness which inspired the "Holy, holy, holy" of Gregorian chant; the cries of the prophets for justice and the gentle strains of God's love for His sinful people: "How can I give you up, O Ephraim?", which tell of the immense depths of the divine heart from which the Gospel message burst forth; and many more things besides . . .

But it is only at the price of unremitting patience that the Christian will make such discoveries. Surrounding the favored passages, the springs of living water, there will be texts that take him over difficult terrain, and it will not be long before the

Old Testament as a whole seems very much like the "great and terrible desert" of which we read in Deuteronomy. For the unprepared Christian, the Old Testament can be—to speak in less imaginative terms—a mine of difficulties and disappointments, stumbling blocks, weariness: the repetitions and the apparent contradictions in an imbroglio of texts, the curious moralizing (the reader wonders whether it is mythical? legendary?) in certain stories, the sometimes totally incomprehensible allusions, the poetry whose secret has been lost, the jokes whose savor has disappeared; and then the brutal or scarcely edifying tales where God's own witnesses are easily the equals of the uncircumcised in trickery or violence, happily cursing their enemies and slaughtering whole cities in the name of Yahweh; and then—hardly shocking, but boring to tears—endless chronologies and lessons in geography, fine points of barbarous ritual, interminable architect's estimates on tent or temple . . . And where is the Word of God?

The inevitable question. There will be some—assured by their faith that the Word of God is present throughout the Old Testament, but still disappointed by the poverty of the literal meaning alone—who will be tempted to plead the "hidden meaning" of Holy Scripture. Their effort to find, under the letter, the spirit which the letter can reveal certainly seems to have a religious motivation. And yet there are grounds for suspecting that such an effort conceals a subtle lack of docility to the spirit as well as to the letter. The notion of a hidden meaning, along with a special method (more or less explicitly set forth) for discovering it, seems to imply a highly individualized approach to the Bible, one which is expected to provide the key which will make all biblical texts readily understandable. The trouble is that the

100

Old Testament itself might resist this sort of approach. In the last analysis, the fact that "spiritual exegesis" is used only for the Bible does not by any means provide *a priori* proof that it befits the Bible: it is not for us to decide that the texts of Scripture demand special treatment in order to be understood. But neither does this fact provide proof that "spiritual exegesis" is less human (and "too human") than any other type of exegesis.

Generally speaking, the use of today's techniques for understanding any human text—literal exegesis—in order to hear the Word of God in the Bible can be every bit as indicative of docility and respect for that Word. Nathanael was affronted by the human origin of Christ: "Can anything good come out of Nazareth?" — "Come and see," is Philip's reply. If the Word of God wanted to be—rather than some sort of direct contact with the ineffable, imprinted in words in the depths of the heart—a human word, spoken to men and lived by men, repeated by men in words of Hebrew and Greek, passed on to still other men "in many and various ways," all we have to do is go and see. With men's eyes. Surely it will not put too much of a strain on man's marvelous abilities—knowledge of language, knowledge of history, literary criticism—to help faith grasp, in these very texts, its own object. We shall simply have to take account of the many witnesses and evaluate and distinguish their different modes of expression if we want to hear the Word of God, with assurance and clarity, in them and through them. Only at the conclusion of a long human relationship with the Master could Peter say what neither flesh nor blood had revealed to him: "You are the Christ, the Son of the living God."

Our first step will be to find our way around in the immense variety of Old Testament writings, to learn how to distinguish

101

the great many authors, known or unknown, who sang, delivered, wrote, compiled, corrected the texts whose disparity is so astonishing. We will acquire familiarity with "the Yahwist" and "the Elohist," with Isaiah and Ezekiel, with the scriveners of Proverbs, with Qoheleth and the author of Job. Rather than getting their voices confused, we will gradually find each one to be like a much-visited teacher with whose way of thinking and of speaking we are perfectly at home, whom we all but instinctively understand. If inspiration is, like God, unique, it is also as many-sided as the men whom God inspired. Short of the beatific vision, we do not read the Bible "over the shoulder" of the Spirit who inspired it; we do not lay hold of inspiration at its source and know the design of God in the unity of divine thought. The course that we must follow is to rise to the crest of inspiration by means of the very texts which bring inspiration down to us. We hear the Word of God in a human word. No *faithful* reading of Scripture can bypass with impunity the conditions of any *exact human* reading—conditions which conduce to a certain *communion* with the author.

It all comes down to "knowing what speech means." But "what speech means" is not exactly the same thing when the speaker is the uncivilized singer of the Canticle of Deborah or the much-later scrivener of Chronicles, when the speaker is documenting the intrigues of David's court, drawing up a code of laws, when the speaker is uttering ecstatically, or endlessly polishing a well-turned maxim. Literal exegesis performs an indispensable function by helping us to see what the different authors, divinely inspired as they were, wanted to say. Literal exegesis does this by making us acquainted with them in all the diversity of their era, their personalities, their tendencies— surrounded by the living community which supported them, which found in them the expression of itself or even the sign of contradiction.

Now we can see how stimulating for faithful study is the disconcerting variety of the Old Testament writings. The Old Testament does not offer us a single voice, reciting from one end to the other a lesson with which we are already familiar, but a hundred contrasting voices, in harmony, in opposition, in transposition, a hundred men's voices over the course of ten centuries, communicating experience, knowledge, and ideas which cannot be reduced to a single denominator. Among them there are historians and epic poets, pilgrims of the absolute and fastidious judges, mystics and sages. "In many and various ways": all the strings of the lyre were needed to sing of the works of God. The ear must accustom itself to recognize the tone of each, the harmonies and the dissonances, so that the heart will hear the unique, ineffable note. Once we have learned to see the mark of an age and the seal of genius in the strange fashions of speaking and thinking of the biblical authors, we will appreciate how closely connected they are with the revelation which they bring to us. It may not be the revelation we had imagined, nor the revelation we had broken down into our own categories, but it will be the revelation of Him who is not the God of philosophers (nor even of theologians), but the God of Abraham, of Isaac, of Jacob, and of each of their sons. This is how literal exegesis, in better distinguishing the characteristics of the Bible's many authors, leads to communion with them. It breaks down our ready-made syntheses and makes room for the many-sided revelation of the Old Testament. It refuses to reduce to univocal categories the diverse and relative modes of expression which it finds there, and thus safeguards the sense of mystery.

If we turn now to the *content* of the Old Testament, we immediately perceive another of its characteristics: like the rest of the Bible, before all else it is a *history,* sacred history.

A history in which God acts is, of course, as disconcerting to us as a human language in which God speaks. The intervention of the "Eternal" in time, as revealed to us by sacred history, can encourage us to consider that history too hastily "under the appearance of the eternal," to fabricate a sacred history which follows a flawless dialectic, a sacred history in which the beginning was already conscious of (and revelatory of) the end, in which the distances of time were abolished by the timeless idea of an immutable design of God. The stories in the Old Testament would ultimately possess no consistency for us other than their "hidden meaning"—the design of God, manifested in the Gospel, and necessarily to be rediscovered in the ancient texts.

Here again, the Old Testament assumes the task of undeceiving us and of reminding us of our human condition: sacred history is true history, and in true history we cannot look down on time. And here again, literal exegesis, by taking the development of this history in time seriously—according to the exact indications of the text—, allows us to grasp its true religious significance with greater fidelity.

Literal exegesis does this first by restoring the proper consistency to each of the events which make up this history—the families, the cities embattled or destroyed, the migrations, the conflicts, the loves, unquestionably constitute the stages of a collective and purposeful movement, directed by God, a "salvation history" which transcends the immediate actors. But these events, in their historical reality (as we can grasp it in the sometimes elaborate and transposed image given by the sacred writers), first concerned living men, made their sweat, their tears, and their blood to run, their hearts to beat with a vague hope or a fleeting passion—and without them there would be no "salvation history" at all. Underlying all the philosophies and all the theologies of history, there is history itself, made up of freedom and fatality, studded over by the holy and weighted down by formless masses, sparked by indomitable forces and stifled by absurd delays. The interventions of God which are thereby revealed, far from contributing a bit of order, add to all these contingencies a sovereign and no less disconcerting freedom, a freedom which loved Jacob and hated Esau. Providence is not the single throw of the dice which does away with chance once and for all. And even the redemptive design, far from being the key presented on the last page which deciphers everything that went before—as in a bad detective story—, is shown to us throughout the course of time, in its "mystery." If we would understand something about it, we must enter into communion with those who experienced it in their own lives, our "fathers in the faith." Then the design will appear to us not as a formula, but as a promise ever-renewed, a promise ever-achieved and ever-deferred, ever more deeply engraved on the hearts of the men who bear it; not as a formula but as a Covenant twenty times broken and twenty times renewed; not as a formula but as a passionate and jealous Love, ever vulnerable and ever victorious, which no deluge could extinguish.

But if sacred history in its actual unfolding remains, despite all our efforts at simplification, subject to the carnal conditions of every human history, the same thing is true of the awareness, given by God to His witnesses and His people, of the significance of this history, of the revelation of His design for them. Attention to the exact meaning of the texts and to their dates and inter-relationships makes it perfectly plain that time has its own role to play in this revelation. The revelation is a progressive one—provided we strip the word "progressive" of the notion of a linear and uniformly ascending development and include in it inconsistency and delay, and the anguished question before an ever obscure enigma, and the cry of hope which goes before certainty. The Old Testament writers, as sacred history moved forward and the promises of God became more explicit or passed into apparent oblivion, never ceased to "rethink" that history, to reflect upon its promises, to see in it the hopes and the disappointments of the nation as well as the secret drama of their own existence. There is, then, not a single biblical theology. There are biblical theologies, more or less tentatively asserting the mystery of God, the providential meaning of Israel's history, the messianic expectation, the hope in the face of death . . . The "divine pedagogy" does not make the same good students pass from one biblical theology to another, as from an "elementary course" to an "advanced course," for in every generation there are others who sometimes docilely repeat the lessons already learned and sometimes forget the old lessons and learn new ones—and there are even some "difficult souls" who question absolutely everything: see Qoheleth, for example.

The Old Testament, then—not as we would have written it, but as it is in fact written. Thus, in its many-sided and fluid reality, arose the "expectation of Israel." And thus was prepared, for the new Israel, the great lesson of waiting, now and always valid "after the birth of Christ." "All the Old Testament speaks of Christ." Certainly. But not as a coded text would speak to one who had the key. More simply, and more divinely—as thirst speaks of water.

III.

The Demands of Translation.
The Psalms

In the final analysis, the demands which must be satisfied by any translation all come down to one: fidelity. It is to bestow on a now-unintelligible collection of signs new value as truth, but not a truth other than its *own* truth. It is to render life to a "dead letter," but its *own* life. The very truth and the very life which the text had for those who wrote it and may still have for certain others. The truth of some texts is no more than local and transitory, and it cannot "cross the Pyrenees" without becoming error. Too bad: correction and adaptation are not the business of a translator. The life of some texts has been extinguished and cannot be restored in a new environment. Too bad: the translator has no right to give it a new kind of life. Yet the great texts live forever.

Translation of biblical texts is no different. Fidelity always remains the same basic demand, but "fidelity" takes on a new and stronger meaning. For the truth and life which must be transmitted in this case, the truth and life of the Bible, do not stem solely from the men who wrote the Bible. They also stem from God who inspired it. At one and the same time, the Bible is Word of God and human word. The reader of the Bible and the translator of the Bible must be faithful both to man *and to God*.

However it is an error to think that *two* fidelities are involved, to imagine that attention to the Word of God and attention to human language can be separated, much more put in opposition, whether in the reading or in the translation of the Bible. Actually, we do see certain readers, supposedly religious, who claim to have a personal and living dialogue with the Word of God, even though they have little interest in the human characteristics of the word and the precise import of those characteristics. We see others, supposedly "matter-of-fact," answering the thousand-and-one problems presented by the biblical texts with a huge arsenal of philological and historical data, but never confronting the mystery of God in those texts. Both groups are unfaithful to the truth of the Bible, hence to the object of their quest. For what is true of the sacraments is also true of the Bible: that which is signified is inseparable from the sign, and divine grace is inseparable from human activity.

We should also acknowledge the fact that—though it does not go as far as that sort of divorce—a stubborn mistrust frequently keeps the faithful (or their pastors) and the exegetes at a distance in regard to Scripture. Let us take an example which brings us very close to our present subject: it is by no means rare to see fervent readers of the Bible who are virtually indifferent to rigorous accuracy in the translation they read, and are even afraid of the "distraction," the "curiosity" inimical to *lectio divina*, they are convinced would flow from clarification of the precise meaning of the texts which could be provided by an exact translation or by the translator's own notes. What they are looking for in the Bible is the Word of God; thinking that they find it there, the scrupulous care of a good translator in weighing words and contexts strikes them as unduly removed from what is essential and as of importance only for an "intermediary" which must be left behind.

But the human language of the Bible can no more be "left behind" than the sacramental sign.[1] The translator, the faithful interpreter, remains an indispensable companion all through our *lectio divina*. The Word of God, in itself, does of course leave him behind, does elude him, just as invisible grace eludes the minister of the sacrament. In its origin, as it springs forth from Silence, and in its end, as it echoes mysteriously in the soul who hears it, the Word of God cannot be translated into any language and has no need of a translation. But to ascend to this origin, to arrive at this end, there is no other road for the mind of man to follow than the one which the Spirit of God himself selected to link together the two poles: the road of human language. "Who spoke through the prophets." There is no other way to hear God than to listen to the men whom He inspired, to enter with them into the communion of language. We must, therefore, know the language these men spoke—or at least have friends who do. Péguy was sorry that he could not read the Old Testament in Hebrew, "hear the Bible as a Jew," as he expressed it. But he added, "I have friends who hear it. And I hear them hearing it."

This is the exegete's indispensable task, both humble and exalted, in the Church. Neither Father nor Doctor, he is nonetheless the friend, "the friend of the bridegroom, who stands and hears him," and he is our friend too. By translating, by faithfully making human words heard again, just as they were

[1] Or the humanity of Christ. St. Teresa of Avila tells how, at the start of her spiritual life, she thought that the humanity of Christ was an intermediary which prayer, at a later stage, would leave behind so as to address the Trinity directly; and how she saw her error: the spiritual life can never do without Christ in His humanity.

spoken and not otherwise, he delivers the Word of God to us, *the Word of God itself and not another word,* such as we might invent or transpose in our own imaginations. The attention he devotes to perceiving exactly "what speech means," what speech meant for the men in the past, who spoke "in former times and in different ways," is not some vain historical curiosity. It is an absolute requirement for authentic religious understanding of the Bible. His scruples about literal fidelity are related to fidelity pure and simple.

If the body of the faithful must be called to a more direct knowledge of the Bible, it seems to us that the "biblical movement" will truly succeed only through renewed contact and discussion between the Christian people and the exegetes (principally, of course, through the mediation of priests with pastoral responsibilities). If the average Christian must more and more find an introduction to Holy Scripture in the liturgical gathering itself, it is most important that the biblical readings during this gathering, the biblical melodies which express its prayer, and the homilies which comment on both, all meet the basic demand of fidelity. The Christian people are entitled to the Bible exactly as it is.

A difficulty crops up here. Priests who have pastoral responsibilities might express it by saying that what they want above all is a Bible "which our people understand." But this desire can be taken in two different ways, not equally acceptable, and we must distinguish them.

Is it meant to indicate that the exegete, in his translations (and in his exegesis, inasmuch as it acquires a pastoral echo), should speak the people's language rather than Canaanite slang? Obviously, and we mention this only to be able to point out a primary truth: to translate one language into another, both languages must be known. Yet it would be easy to find general support for the proposition that translators do forget their mother tongue. One of the benefits of the renewed contact we have recommended between exegetes and the Christian community should be to remind the exegetes of their need to be understood by that community, and to put their translations to the indispensable test of use, and public use in particular. This should be done, however, on the condition that the trial be long enough to be conclusive, that words or expressions will not too hastily be rejected as incomprehensible merely because, though still assimilable, they are mysterious, and that the possibility of enriching the mental and verbal universe of "our people," through the Bible itself, is not ruled out.

This leads us to a consideration of the second way in which we can interpret the desire for a Bible "which our people understand." Is it meant to indicate that the people should be spared any kind of strangeness, that the people should be able to listen to the Bible without finding in it a different climate than they find in sermons or study groups? Here we shall certainly have to draw the line, and be willing to take things just as they are. The Bible may very well not be what we would ourselves have written as the final report of a St. Vincent de Paul Society convention, or even the annual meeting of the Liturgical Conference. There may be things in the Bible which are foreign to our teaching methods, and even our way of understanding liturgical catechesis. But the Bible is like that. Its nourishment may be too rich to be given to the faithful before they have been prepared for it (pastors and faithful alike will digest it only if they themselves are living, and living in the Church for which the Bible is intended). But we have no right to cut it down to our own dimensions. Should we decide to work seriously to make the Bible better known to the faithful, to make it encompass their prayer and their lives, we shall have to expect difficulties, both for our people and for ourselves. These difficulties, however, are the occasion and the condition for new growth and authenticity. The Bible's dimensions are those of the universal Church. Perhaps the Christianity we are living (faithful and priests alike) is too stunted. Then let us grow.[2]

Thus we see that the demand for fidelity which is made of the translator of the Bible must resound through him so as to reach the reader of the Bible. To offer the Bible to the Christian reader in his own language can never be a simple matter of putting the Bible in the reader's "reach," but must be an invitation for him to undertake his own journey into the Bible, to answer a *summons* from truth. What most concerns the translator who strives only for fidelity is not so much the fear of failing to be understood immediately as the fear of failing to make that summons heard.

When it comes to the Psalms, the demand for fidelity takes on two important particulars, by reason of two features which belong to this book more than to any other, although each is shared with many another biblical text.

In the first place, the Psalms are *poetic* texts. The translation must therefore strive to render their poetic essence. It must render the "form" as well as the "content," since the distinction between "form" and "content," deceptive in any case, becomes nonsense in poetry. Anyone who pretended to translate the

[2] St. Augustine puts this exhortation on the lips of the Word: "I am the nourishment of the strong. You will not change me into yourself, as you do with your body's nourishment; but you will be changed into me. Grow and take nourishment from me."

Psalms without trying to grasp and to express the unity of words, their value, their color and their rhythm, the emotion and the thought they contain, would betray not only the beauty but also the truth of the Psalms. (A parable in the Gospels would be betrayed no less if we contented ourselves with giving its "point," and simply omitted the parable itself.) There is no need to emphasize here the problems and advantages which the vernacular language and spirit present to the translator of Hebrew poetry. But we should remember, when we show concern for such things, that we are not dealing with "literary niceties" which are outside the province of a translator of the Bible. Once again, we are simply respecting, on an essential point, the basic requirement of fidelity.[3] By "replacing the poetic with the oratorical, or a particular poetic with another," we would be missing not merely the literary beauty of, but the truth proper to, the Psalms.

In the second place, the Psalms are a book of *prayer*. This gives a special dimension to the demand for fidelity which is made of one who translates the Psalms in and for the Church. It is not enough to render the psalmists' surge of prayer in such a way as to let today's Christian reader know how his fathers prayed. And it is not enough if this ancient prayer, presented to the reader anew, stimulates him to a new prayer. The psalmists' prayer must become his Christian prayer. The Church, after all, as guardian of the Scriptures, has not preserved the Book of

---

[3] This inseparable unity of "content" and "form" in biblical texts (as in all other texts) is basically what is taught by the doctrine of "literary genres," as recognized and approved by the encyclical *Divino Afflante Spiritu*. Recognition of the literary genre of a text is not simply a convenient tool for exegesis, useful in disposing of difficulties related to biblical inerrancy, for example. It is the necessary condition for arriving at the text in its *truth*. The text is not translated by "extracting" its message. The message is *in* the text and is inseparable from it. Consequently, it is the text, flesh and spirit, which must be understood and translated.

113

Psalms as a simple witness to her own history, or even as a Word of God which is merely to be listened to. The Church has preserved the book which was Israel's prayer book as her own prayer book, forever, just as she remains forever the spiritual Israel. The prayer of the Psalms is not yesterday's prayer, but one which is always alive. This is why a translation of the Psalms has *not yet* attained complete fidelity as long as it has not translated prayer into prayer, as long as the Psalm is not, through the translation, once again uttered, sung and sent up to God "in the sight of the Church."

Here, the translator must await the fulfillment of his work from his brethren—it no longer makes sense to say "from his readers." He offers to their living voice the words which he intended to be faithful and which will truly be so only when the voice once again bestows upon them their most secret and most essential truth: the surge of a man, of a community of men, towards God.

The translator's intention is, then, to be of service to his brethren in their very act of prayer. Such a service, though, cannot be forced. It is for the Psalms themselves to exert their infectious power, to create themselves anew as prayer on the lips of those who have heard them—provided the translator (and this is his constant concern) has not, by his own fault, prevented this power from making itself felt. All personal efforts to make the Psalms prayed, however, are strictly forbidden: there must be no personal entreaties, no "helping hand" intended to cause a "sensitive chord" to respond more readily. A moment ago, we said that we must not replace one poetic with another. Now we say that we must not replace one prayer with another. Obviously, the prayer of the Psalms will not always be "natural" for today's Christian, and here again we touch on the inevitable difficulties faced by a serious proposal of the Bible to the faithful. Once the

114

prayer of the Psalms is no longer supported by the Latin of the chant, once it has ceased to be a kind of suspended animation or an individual and individualistic prayer, it may very well seem to be an *obstacle* to prayer. Because it is emotional, and even violent, or because it takes the soul outside itself so as to join it to the world's praise, a world whose sacred character we no longer appreciate, or because it is marked by the events of an actual history, expressive of carnal hopes, because it curses enemies long since dead, or because it bears a mysterious meaning, this prayer of the Psalms can shock, stun, disconcert "regular church-goers." It can make them sea-sick, or air-sick. But to all who, with the help of those in the community who are the leaders of prayer, enter into the prayer of the Psalms, it will open up a new world: heaven and earth, bread and wine, laughter and tears, life and death, war and peace, anguish, expectation, thanksgiving. With all of these they will now pray, and no longer in a corner but in the solidarity of the entire people of God, the kings and the beggars, the sinners and the sages—and the Messiah. The organ in the parish church will accompany the age-old song of Israel.

IV.

The Professors and the Imagination

Truth and Imagination

MAN has no more exalted and no more urgent task than the pursuit of truth, both in thought and in action. So it is perfectly normal for the man who reads the Bible to seek truth in it before anything else. Whether the Bible is considered as God's Word or as man's word, it appeals to that faculty in man which allows him to grasp and to appreciate truth. We may call this faculty intellect, reason, understanding, or whatever we please. But if the Bible is God's Word, we should see that our reading of it, in the faith which acknowledges the divine origin of the sacred text, has not been completely successful until we have "read" within it the mystery of God whom it reveals. *Fides quaerens intellectum.* Faith seeks "understanding" (*intelligere = intus legere*, to read within, to discover the essential truth which is hidden under the words and images). And if the Bible is man's word, it must be subjected to a searching "cross-examination." With faith or without faith, our reading has not been completely successful until our intellect is satisfied that "the Bible told the truth."

116

So it is also perfectly normal for the Bible to have been closely examined by the intellect, for each page of the Bible to have been subjected to the scrutiny of theological reasoning and the criteria of criticism. Each text and each event reported by a text had to be "controlled," made more definite, and the truth had to be extracted from it. The intellect's indispensable tool, "exegetical method," was patiently perfected over the course of centuries—and not without crises. And today, it is generally agreed, we are better equipped than we ever were to discover the Bible's truth.

What is imagination's role in this pursuit? It seems, at first sight, to be an obstacle which must be either hurdled or evaded. At the very best, it strikes us as a temporary prop which should be eliminated with the least possible delay. It is held in suspicion by historical criticism, which much prefers to examine witnesses who are not overburdened with imagination. When they are— and they always are—, it should be "eliminated," so that we can obtain, in a chemically pure state, the historical fact recounted or the "essence" of the message conveyed. If, as appears to be the case, the events of sacred history and the teachings of the Bible have not come down to us in their naked objectivity, but clothed in various "forms" and "literary genres," they must be reduced to that objectivity. So we must distinguish the literary genres and perfect our "form criticism"—compiling the "history of forms." Our task will be to make poetry disclose the prose it contains, and to make prose disclose its precise objective content. Historical criticism can never be at rest until it has "demythologized" the truth from the occurrence.

Theological reasoning, on the other hand, assumes that the rational reduction of texts to their content has already been accomplished. Sometimes it is a bit hasty in making the assumption.

In any event, theological reasoning, though for quite different motives, also exercises a strict control over the imagination. It takes the precept of the Decalogue very seriously: "You shall not make yourself a graven image." It knows full well that the mystery of God far exceeds any perceptible expression, that God's thoughts are not our thoughts, nor God's ways our ways. Naturally, it acknowledges, because it is human reason, its dependence on the senses and imagination, and knows by rote the Aristotelian maxim: *Nihil est in intellectu quod non prius fuerit in sensu*. But the task which it claims for itself is the abstraction of the intelligible, the separation of the pure diamond of "eternal truths" from the matrix of things and images. It cannot be satisfied with metaphor, but insists on the strict proposition of dogma.[1] Undoubtedly, the Bible is filled with images, and the theologian rejects none of them. But the ideal of theological reasoning is to break away from images and extract from them the concept (which must then be purified further by the trick of analogy). As far as theological reasoning is concerned, the imagination is (if we dare speak once again in metaphor) nothing but the "thrust" which assists the take-off of thought— once it has been put into orbit and released from the earth's pull, thought can have no further interest in the imagination.

These precautions and demands of reason are all legitimate and even beneficial. Mature faith not only pays heed to them but finds in them a healthy climate in which to expand in full self-awareness. We do well to refrain from looking for amuse-

[1] The schema *De Ecclesia* which was proposed to the Fathers of the First Vatican Council defined the Church, in quite scriptural terms, as "the mystical body of Christ." We know that the schema was not adopted. It is interesting to note that, among the reasons for its rejection, many of the Fathers found it unseemly to define the Church by a "metaphor." No room for the imagination when it comes to serious business!

ment or easy edification in the Bible, and to concentrate on looking into its *truth*.

Still in all, if we must "go to the truth with our whole soul," we should take care lest we whittle down our soul to what we take to be its fine point, lest we put our soul to work on nothing but its most sophisticated activity. And suppose truth itself appealed not only to the critical intelligence, not only to the spiritual intellect, but to the imagination as well?

The Bible answers this question for us. We have only to read it to become aware of the fact that, despite the demands it puts on the reader's intellectual seriousness and docile faith, the Bible certainly does not dismiss the imagination out of hand. The imagination is needed to read the Bible, because it was needed to write it.

The Bible, a Work of the Imagination

The Bible, the word of truth, is also a work of the imagination. This is so for several reasons. The first and essential reason is that the Bible has *God* as its author. If "style makes the man," the style of the Bible (not the details of its various styles, but its general movement, its harmonies and dissonances) reveals something about the divine Author. It would be hazardous to suggest that it reveals God's imagination, since we dare not conceive of anything like "images" in the divine knowledge. On the other hand, theologians do speak of "divine ideas," though simultaneously proposing all sorts of precautions and correctives when relating them to our own ideas, abstract and accidental as they are. The interesting thing is that we can acquire some slight inkling of the way in which "idea," in God, avoids abstraction and superficial accident, and takes on concreteness, creativity, and subsistence, precisely by referring to what is called "creative imagination" in the artist and the man of action, the quality which is over and above mere clarity of thought. This inventive power, this inability to be reduced to any closed system, this lack of respect for "formal objects," this free play on all the levels of being—in defiance of the laws of balance and of logic, this paradoxical success, this profound coherence and dynamic convergence, transcending contradictions—all these are qualities whose presence we must recognize in the Author of the Bible, both as lived history and as transcribed history, both as "form" and as "content." And the word which does the least inadequate job of evoking all these qualities at once—even as we freely acknowledge that it is something entirely different in God—is, in our language, "imagination."

We will be told that we are projecting this imagination to God because we have encountered it in the Bible, which is the Word of God. We will be told that it happens to be man's word too. The Word of God obviously had to pass through the channel of words, things, and images, but we who receive it must, by the powers of our reason and our faith, grasp it in its unadorned truth, we must ascend to God on the same road which the divine pedagogy travelled down to us. By patient study of the "literary genres," inherited by the biblical authors from the ancient East and in fact transformed by them, we must learn "what speech means to say." Thus we will not be led astray by the glamor of the imagination but will grasp, within the stories, poems, or oracles of the Bible, the "content" which is hidden under a particular "form," the revealed truth which is the only thing that matters to us.

Yes and no. To be sure, the reading of the Bible must remain faithful to the demand for truth which was implanted in us by

God and which must be satisfied by His Word. It is a very serious matter. But can it really succeed without the imagination? No, it cannot. The Bible being what it is (because it is what God willed it to be), we shall discover that the imagination, the notorious "mistress of error," the "castle in the air," is indispensable in the pursuit of biblical truth.

The Bible's Imaginary Realm

There are undoubtedly a number of different ways in which the imagination must enter in as we read the different parts of the Bible, for the Bible itself is something different. It is not simply a book, and still less a carefully organized manual. The Bible, it has been said, is a library, a kind of public archive or "family album," and collections of this sort are not noted for their homogeneity. A good library, after all, contains prose and poetry, novels, books on science, history and politics. Public archives are filled with collections of laws, administrative documents, registers of deeds, registers of vital statistics. And anyone who has rummaged through family records—whether from historical curiosity, or filial piety, or just to try to unearth those unfindable receipts that the Internal Revenue Service insists on—is quite aware of the immense variety of things to be found there: the grandparents' marriage license, the deed to the real estate in the Catskills, newspaper clippings on the 1904 World's Fair, Uncle Clarence's citation for bravery in World War I, Aunt Abigail's love letters, the patent for the pump Cousin Matt invented. From this treasure, the father of the family draws forth old things and new. The different items obviously have very different effects on the imagination. In much the same way, an attentive examination of *"the Bible"* soon uncovers *several* books between the same boards. Within the books themselves, elements are discovered whose variety is somewhat reminiscent of Chesterton's famous "What I Found in My Pocket," or, to take a more fitting comparison, the "net which was thrown into the sea and gathered fish of every kind" (Mt. 13, 47). Let us give a few examples. There are collections of laws (a good portion of the Pentateuch), but the laws run the gamut from an absolute like the Decalogue's "You shall not kill" (Ex. 20, 13) to the details of a penal code: the fixing of compensation for harm caused by a mean-tempered animal (Ex. 21, 35–36). There is history, too, but history which ranges from the clear and colorful chronicle of David's domestic dramas (2 Sam. 9–20; 1 Kgs. 1–2) and the "saga" of Exodus to the detailed travel diary of Luke, Paul's companion (for example, Acts 27–28), and the picaresque adventures of Samson (Jdg. 13–16). There are genealogies (the first chapters of Chronicles), architect's specifications (Ezek. 40–42), and the memoirs of the general contractor (2 Chron. 4, 11–18). There are novelettes (Tobit, Judith, Esther) and there is poetry—poetry as varied as is French poetry from the *Song of Roland* to Rimbaud: the savage song of Deborah and Barak (Jdg. 5), the tragic poem of Job, psalms of distress and psalms of glory, the love lyrics of the Song of Songs. There is "wisdom": tiny well-polished proverbs and questions without an answer; the traditional wisdom of Sirach and the "beatnik" wisdom of Ecclesiastes. There are the Prophets: "The Word of Yahweh was addressed to" Moses, Elijah, Amos, Hosea, Isaiah, Jeremiah; and we discover that the unique Word is every bit as diverse as Moses, Elijah, Amos, Hosea, Isaiah, Jeremiah. And, of course, the Gospels, their sources and the purposes served by their arrangement, purposes which a careful study of the synoptics and of John will reveal.

A triple lesson is to be learned from this variety. In the first place, it helps us to grasp, as we have already pointed out, the "something" in God Himself, in the revelation made to men by God, which we dared not call the divine imagination. In the second place, it demonstrates, on the level where the Word of God becomes man's word in the Bible, that this Word makes liberal use of the imaginative powers of the witnesses whom the Word inspires. But the use is varied in intensity and extent. Inspiration sometimes leads the one who is inspired into the realm of facts, unadorned and lacking in imagery, which must be reported just as they are, or into the realm of commands, which permit no freedom of interpretation. Sometimes, too, the witness, convinced that he has "visions," is led by the Lord to the simple establishment of the facts: "But they were startled and frightened, and supposed that they saw a spirit. And he said to them, '. . . See my hands and my feet, that it is I myself; handle me and see; for a spirit has not flesh and bones as you see that I have'" (Lk. 24, 37–39). On the other hand, inspiration sometimes gives free rein to the inspired author's imagination, and then we can observe him embellishing his canvas in all sorts of ways, showing off his technical skill, and even (if we dare say it) "adding a bit"—we can see a typical example of the latter by comparing the "plague of darkness" in Egypt as recounted in Ex. 10, 21–23 and as expanded upon in the *midrash* of Wisd. 17, 1–18, 4. Between the two extremes, divine inspiration makes use of all possible combinations of human imagination, in greater or lesser intensity, with the other constituents of knowledge: understanding and intellect, theoretical or practical, memory, invention, tradition; and to do this it makes use of all the modes of thinking and writing which were familiar in the ancient East and adds a few more as well.

Reading the Bible Imaginatively

All this points up the third aspect of the lesson taught by the Bible's diversity. The imaginative power, whose origin we suspect in God and whose activity we see in the biblical writers, must not remain dormant in the *reader* of the Bible. If we wish to go to the truth promised by the Bible with all the powers of our soul, we cannot allow the resources of the imagination to remain idle. This is not simply a matter of "taking heed" of their power, in order to avoid being carried away by their fancifulness, or so as to be able to reduce the images of the Bible to their intelligible "solid marrow" through sound criticism and theological reasoning. What it means is that we must make the positive use of the imagination's resources that God Himself did not disdain, that we must become *personally* aware of the vast imaginative realm of the Bible, that we must explore it and make it our own *by* the imagination.

The imagination actually plays a number of roles. Situated at several levels of knowledge, it can, depending on circumstances, be undesirable (as a distraction); it can be useful, though in relative and transient fashion; and it can be absolutely necessary, and in permanent fashion. We must evaluate each of these aspects on its own merits.

First of all, the imagination is a *stimulant* for the intellect. It arouses the attention. If someone were to read *Through the Looking Glass* to me, I would find it delightful. But a clever professor, after reading it to me, could easily bring me back to "serious matters": "Why don't you ask what became of the Knight?" The divine Wisdom has not looked down on such modest and effective pedagogy, but freely tells us stories and occasionally

124

uses the modern techniques of "suspense" (see the vicissitudes of the story of Joseph, Gen. 37–45).

In addition to simply arousing the attention, the imagination aids the intellect by furnishing it with a *concrete form* to work with, and from which to grasp a truth. The story which we are told "makes us think," and the image which we are offered gives a certain orientation to intellectual insight. A lesson "is extracted" from the story, an idea "is extracted" from the image. But without the story or the image, thought would never have taken wing. In this way, the imagination assumes for the intellect the kind of temporary usefulness we see in the "first-stage rocket," placing the intellect in a particular orbit where it can thereafter, without images, gravitate according to its own laws. Historical criticism and theological reasoning have a job to do here: what they must do is separate the "satellite" from the "rocket," and send the imagination off to burn its wings in the thick layers of the atmosphere; they must "extract" from the concrete form which it possesses in the biblical text the irreducible fact which pertains to the salvation-event, or the real notion which allows us to grasp from afar something of God's mystery. The literary form of a story must, therefore, be studied, and there must be an appreciation of the role played in it by the imagination (the role is one which varies with the subject matter: a direct chronicle like 2 Sam. 9–20, or a treatment of oral traditions as in the saga of Abraham, or a blend of epic tales like those of Exodus). But the object of this study is not to "eliminate" the imaginary as much as it is to discover its relationship with the real, to discover the technique which connects the imaginary with the event and thereby reveals its reality to us. Similarly, "form criticism" will prove its value when it gives us a better grasp of the irreducible truth of the Gospel accounts through our analysis of the more or less "stereotyped" forms given to them by Christian catechesis.[2] Further, but this time on the level of theological reasoning, we shall certainly have to go beyond the image when we read, for example, that "God repented" of the evil which He intended to do His people. The Bible itself requires this of us by teaching us also that in God "there is no variation or shadow due to change" (Jas. 1, 17). The "repentance of God" can then be seen as the revealed image which suggests that we keep together, within the divine simplicity (and with the combined-resources offered to our intellect by the *via causalitatis,* the *via remotionis,* and the *via eminentiae*), the contrary demands of justice and mercy.

But this is not all. In human knowledge, the imagination plays more than this auxiliary and transitory role. As we have said, the imagination provides the intellect with the concrete form from which it can extract what is true. We should take heed of the fact that there are vast areas in the field of human knowledge where this task of "extraction" is *never* completed.[3] The image then becomes the permanent guardian of the truth which it contains. By rejecting the image, we would lose the truth.

The Imagination as Power of Truth

The need for the imagination is especially apparent in those areas where knowledge would remain imperfect without some

[2] When the intellect undertakes these analyses and controls, it must, of course, do so with intellectual honesty and not become an imagination-in-reverse, making *a priori* assumptions, using hypotheses whose hypothetical character is soon lost sight of, using unverified analogies . . .

[3] In the preceding example, for instance, what would be left of the intellectual reconciliation of the divine attributes (justice and mercy) if their *exercise* were not *concretely* apparent in the numerous historical "repentances" of God which lend support to the intellectual construct?

presence of the object: human presence, divine presence, presence of those realities in which man and God meet. Intellectual abstraction, which knows nothing of presence, would in such cases permit the concrete reality to escape unless it had the help of the senses, the memory, or the imagination. When the lawyer asks him, "What shall I do to inherit eternal life?", Jesus answers in the precept of the Law: "You shall love the Lord your God . . . and your neighbor as yourself." But the other, "desiring to justify himself," makes the casuistic retort: "And who is my neighbor?" We know the answer: "A man was going down from Jerusalem to Jericho . . ." To make the intellect confront the truth about man head-on, man must be *imagined*. The good Samaritan—there is your neighbor.

The same thing is true of the revelation of the "kingdom." What is the use of defining it unless it first *exists* for us? Now "the kingdom of heaven is like" a mustard seed, a lamp, a net. The intellect grasps the "point" of the parable and is able to translate it into explicit terms. But what would become of the idea if the image were not there to lend support? What would we know about the kingdom if we did not have the parables of the Lord, or if, once we had heard them, we lost no time in forgetting them, concerned only with preserving their "point"? What would we know about the kingdom if we reduced the mysteries of God to abstract ideas? Truth is *in* the image rather than in the idea we can draw from it.

Among those special areas in which imagination remains the condition for knowledge, we must include the field of history. We know perfectly well that if we were to ask Professors Langlois and Seignobos for a definition of *history*, we would be offered a notion in which the imagination, even if not completely absent, would be under rigid control. How different a notion we would draw from the tales of the old lady who is asked, "Grandma, tell me a *story*." In point of fact, real historical knowledge is likely to be somewhere between "history" and "story," for it is neither the tale made up *for* the imagination nor the "objective" science made up of facts from which all imagination has supposedly been stripped. How, after all, can we expect to make contact with the past—which will be a truly human past and not simply its reduction to a collection of dates and propositions devoid of meaning—unless we somehow rediscover the *presence* of the men who lived it?[4] And how can we find these men again unless we relive their past with them through our imagination (supported by well-documented facts, the documents themselves being sensibly "interpreted")? If it is important that history strictly verify the events of which it treats, it is no less important that it treat them as events, that it "participate" in them, and that it somehow become that "resurrection of the past" on which Michelet put so much insistence. The ways which ensure success in such a project are many, just as the past lives on for the spirit in various ways—from official records to myths. The imagination has its role in each of them. In order to embrace the past, the reader's imagination must be in harmony with the writer's imagination.

If we cannot come to a knowledge of history without the imagination, it is still clearer that we can have no "understanding" of poetry without the imagination. We simply have not understood a poem when we have merely translated verse into prose and image into idea. The image is what remains present in the poetic memory and introduces the mind into a sphere of knowledge which is more exalted and more concrete than that

[4] See H. I. Marrou, *The Meaning of History*, London and Baltimore, 1956.

of the concept. This is all so obvious that we are almost ashamed to repeat it. And yet, how many commentaries on the Bible, how many patient professors strive earnestly to neutralize the explosive power of images, to reduce to the modest categories of the intellect the lyrical themes of psalmists and prophets!

The Life of Imaginary Forms

The obscurities of an unknown world might provide some excuse for the professors. If so many texts disclose their truth only to the imagination, the imagination's road to truth is not very likely to be an easy one. Like the stars or like radioactive atoms, the concrete forms offered to the mind by the image live and die. There is a "life of forms" (Henri Focillon), and it is a life with mysterious laws. Images die too. Images which had a powerful impact on the imagination of a particular age or civilization may have no meaning whatever for men of a later era or men who are subject to different conditions of existence. An anthology of world humor provides the most ardent lover of national jokes with a good many opportunities not to laugh. The passage of fifty years may be sufficient to make an artistic or literary work which enkindled an era incapable of interesting anyone at all. Centuries later, the work may sometimes find unexpected affinity with a new sensibility.

Biblical forms are not immune from this law. It has become a commonplace to point out that the biblical images conveyed by the Catholic liturgy no longer have anything to say to the men of today's technical civilization. The generalization is one which stands in need of a few distinctions. "Biblical images," for example, neatly conceals an area which is far too vast (as we have seen) to be covered by so all-embracing a judgment. Even so, the generalization is useful in boldly drawing attention to a common and continuing problem, that of communication. Is there a fundamental imaginary world which underlies all the variations, a world which is as constant as human nature? Or have certain forms of the imagination definitively ceased to be viable, like the dinosaur? Whatever the answer might be, each generation possesses its own spontaneous imagination. The creations of preceding generations, if they still have something to say to later ones, will do so only at the cost of a considerable effort of translation and introduction, will do so, that is to say, only through a culture.

But if a culture is made up of information, it is also made up of sympathy. Erudition is not culture. True culture does not exist without generosity, without willing openness to others, without a sense of universal brotherhood. Thus we see that living faith (which blossoms into love for God and love for neighbor) is no less necessary for an imaginative reading of the Bible than it is for a theological reading. Like the intellect, the imagination needs the evangelical *metanoia*. It must go out of itself and its own little garden and enter into communion with God, with the prophets and the apostles, with the men of all ages and the men of our own. "Unless a grain of wheat falls into the earth and dies, it remains alone."

CONCLUSION

ENCOUNTER WITH CHRIST

The Source and End of Scripture

No one has ever seen God; the only Son, who is in the bosom of the Father, he has made him known (Jn. 1, 18).

IF we know God, we know Him in and through Christ, who brings the Word of God to us. Christ, in His person and in His activity, reveals to us the being and the life of God. "And the Word became flesh and dwelt among us, . . . we have beheld his glory" (Jn. 1, 14). Christ, of whom we speak, is among us. Each of us knows Him, of course. But how do we know Him?

We are Members of a Race

We can all remember words or passages from men who knew Christ before we did. We think, for example, of Lacordaire's wonderful exclamation after his discovery that Christ alone can be loved eternally: "One day we pause for a moment and listen, and a voice deep within us says: There is Jesus Christ!" Christ Himself spoke to us about the men who had recognized Him. We become conscious of a hidden emotion and a source of spiritual peace when, surrounded by those who had rejected Him, He is heard to declare, "Your father Abraham rejoiced that he was to see my day; he saw it and was glad" (Jn. 8, 56). Peter's outcry is no different: "Without having seen him you love him; though you do not now see him you believe in him and rejoice with unutterable and exalted joy" (1 Pet. 1, 8). The same faith is implicit in Revelation's final confession, which sums up all the others: "The Spirit and the Bride say, 'Come.' And let him who hears say 'Come'" (Rev. 22, 17).

We, in our turn, also know Christ. We come after Abraham, after the prophets and the apostles (witnesses of the messianic hope and witnesses pure and simple); after four centuries of Christological controversy and several councils, after twenty centuries of theology and exegesis, after innumerable attempts to write "The Life of Jesus" and almost as many "Treatises on Christ," after years devoted to study of them, after how many mystical reunions and dialogues; after an immense throng of men who spent their lives making the sign of the cross with Him. And still, after all our years as baptized Christians—and, if we are priests, after all the Masses in which we have lent Him our hands and our voices, "in memory of me"—and after all that we have preached in His name, the question is asked: What image do we have of Christ? What do we know about Him? What is He to us?

It cannot be denied that each one of us is still being asked the question: "Who do men say that the Son of Man is? . . . But who do you say that I am?" (Mt. 16, 13. 15).

Here above all must each one of us give his own answer. It is the same answer and it is a different answer, just as John, Peter, Matthew, or Paul said things which were the same and yet were different. It is each one's secret. Like Nathanael, each of us has a fig tree, where Christ came to look for him.

Following These Witnesses

We can do no better than to follow these witnesses. This, of course, is just what is asked of us, but we are not convinced of it firmly enough. We must move constantly forward, must make a progressive voyage of discovery. No one questions the fact that we know our catechism: two natures, one person, of course —but *how* do we know it? We should ask the question of ourselves before we ask it of our brethren. In order to understand it a little better, we can try to see how it was that His disciples— those who saw Him: Peter, John, Andrew, Zacchaeus, Magdalene, Paul—knew Christ, whom they had *seen*. One day, a vocation had come to each of them, whether they received a simple call—"follow me"—, or witnessed a miracle, or heard His words, or had Christ Himself come looking for them under the fig tree, or had been pardoned of their sins, or had had Christ pointed out to them by John the Baptist. Faith was born on each of these occasions, though it may often have been something other than faith at the start, something like the astonishment or the sense of wonder that made the crowds murmur, "It is Elijah, or one of the prophets."

The example given by these witnesses helps us to see what it will mean for us, to see more clearly that it may be little more than a stirring within, a discovery, calling us to follow Him. And yet, Jesus preached that the kingdom began by a dramatic break with the old and an opening onto something new: "The time is fulfilled, and the kingdom of God is at hand; repent, and believe in the gospel" (Mk. 1, 15). The witnesses fall in line, even though the demons are quicker of mind: "I know who you are, the Holy One of God" (Mk. 1, 24), and the people, filled with fear, still ask one another questions: "They were all amazed, so that they questioned among themselves, saying 'What is this? A new teaching! With authority he commands . . .'" (Mk. 1, 27). But through all the resistance, and the "messianic murmurings," faith pursues its path towards knowledge. Now they have met Christ; later they will learn, day by day, to know Him. It is a bit like the dialogue between Rodrigo and the Chinese Servant in Claudel's *The Satin Slipper:* "Recognition? Tell me even the colour of her eyes!"

Christ's Gradual Embrace

This faith will make its way forward through *questions.* While the storm rages, Christ sleeps. Who then is He? (Mk. 1, 35–41). For us as well as for themselves, the disciples made this journey, this "cogitation of faith" which St. Thomas Aquinas will speak of, this quest of faith in pursuit of its object.

In the Gospel, we gradually discover the *human features* of the Christ whom the disciples met: pity, anger, tears, weariness.

We follow the disciples in the discovery of *power,* the witnessing of miracles, the encounter with authoritative utterance. This was how they discovered the habits of God in the behavior of a man, "taking the form of a servant, being born in the likeness of men" (Phil. 2, 7).

And thus right up to *Peter's confession:* "You are the Christ, the Son of the living God" (Mt. 16, 13–16).

Immediately ("From that time . . . ," Mt. 16, 21), the announcement of the *passion* brings with it a new source of scandal and prompts Christ's utterance: "You are not on the side of God, but of men" (Mt. 16, 23).

The *transfiguration* then assumes all its significance, as the seal of divinity impressed on humanity destined for death (Mt. 17, 1 ff). "And they were on the road, going up to Jerusalem" (Mk. 10, 32).

Then the *decisive crisis of the passion:* what is left of their faith now? The pilgrims on the road to Emmaus tell us, "But we had hoped that he was the one to redeem Israel. Yes, and besides all this, it is now the third day since this happened" (Lk. 24, 21). But there is something more: "Did not our hearts burn within us while he talked to us on the road, while he opened to us the scriptures?" (Lk. 24, 32). Something always remains of what we have *believed,* though it be night. Our own faith is at times rather like that. . . .

And finally the risen Christ—from now on, faith is certain, but the certainty dwells in mystery. Romano Guardini has an excellent discussion of it in his book *The Lord*—Christ actually alive, but not as familiar as He once was. The mystery is one of presence and distance, and is treated extremely well by St. Thomas Aquinas in the questions on the life of the risen Christ: "The resurrection was both true and glorious": "Put your finger here, and see my hands; and put out your hand, and place it in my side" (Jn. 20, 27). But also: "Do not hold me" (Jn. 20, 17).

Thus opens out before us the journey which will lead us to the mystery of Christ which faith must confront. For us, the content of this faith has been established by Scripture, the councils, the theologians, and we can surely say that we "know" who Christ is.

We "know"? When we read the entire Bible, we see all that this word required of the disciples:

—from familiarity ("we who have eaten and taken drink with him") to adoration;

—from confidence ("Lord, if it is you, bid me come to you on the water") to fear ("Lord, depart from me, I am a sinful man");

—from "we will go and die with him" or Peter's protestations, to slumber in the garden of Gethsemane and eventual flight;

—from "I do not know the man" to "I give you what I have; in the name of Jesus Christ of Nazareth, walk" (Acts 3, 6);

—from "Who will be first in your kingdom?" to "Then they left the presence of the council, rejoicing that they were counted worthy to suffer dishonor for the name" (Acts 5, 41).

For us twentieth-century Christians too, whether we be trained theologians or simple members of the faithful, belief in Christ and the following of Christ may make it necessary to pass over all these roads. Our "brethren in the faith" have built this house with the sweat of their brow. The sons dwell at ease within it ... and saying "Lord my friend" is sometimes just a bit too easy.

Faith was a spiritual struggle for Christ's witnesses—there is no "Daddy's boy" in the kingdom of heaven. Faith is going to be an interior struggle (possibly an exterior struggle as well) for us too. Can we meet its demands? It is here that we enter into mystery.

If we do know the living Christ during our own lives, contemplation must constantly renew our faith in the Mystery of Christ, Jesus the Lord: "Lord, it is you," I know you and I know you not. . . . Let my faith be a living faith, and so I may embrace you and be embraced by you.

Index

Aristotelian, 118
Articles of faith, God revealed in,
  23
Augustine, St., 19, 112 n. 2
Authenticity of biblical text, 34 n.
  5

Barthian, 83 n. 1
Benoit, P., 32 n. 4
Bible, the, 19, 23, 61
  authentic interpretation of, 47
  as book of Christ, 62–65
  as book of the Church, 45, 66–
    69
  as book of prayer, 75–78
  and Christ, 16
  and the Christian, 66
  and Christian culture, 18
  and the Church's teaching, 16
  how to read, 13, 33ff., 61
  as human word, 28f., 107
  inerrancy of, 34, 36ff.
  inspired by God, 28
  as "living water," 19–20
  meaning and meanings of, 21,
    38–45, 95
    accommodated, 44
    anagogical, 42
    Christic, 42
    literal, 39ff., 43, 97
    moral, 42
    scriptural, 44
    spiritual, 43

    tropological, 42
  as "mirror," 19, 70–74, 77
  mystery of, 28, 30, 37
  as promise, 58–61
  reading of, 13–18, 49–51
    consecutive, 49
    critical, 50
    difficulties in, 22ff.
    not forbidden, 16
    imaginative, 124f.
    literal, 38, 97
    liturgical, 50
    not obligatory, 15–16
    poetic, 51
    recommended, 16
    spiritual, 38, 50f.
    not a substitute for other re-
      ligious activities, 47
    theological, 50
  as sacred history, 45, 55–57
  senses of, 24
  and tradition, 46, 95
  translation of, 16, 107ff.
  truth of, 21
  "wilderness of," 20ff.
  as Word of God, 22, 28f., 31, 33,
    35, 55ff., 77, 107, 116
Biblical movement, 91ff., 99

Chifflot, T. G., 39 n. 6
Christian,
  calling of, 60f.
  as practicing theologian, 23

Christian life, well-springs of, 17
Church,
    apostolic mission of, 82
    unity of, 16
Claudel, Paul, 24, 25, 51, 136
"Cogitation of faith," 23
Corneille, Pierre, 40
Council of Florence, 28
Criticism, biblical, 86, 117
Cullmann, Oscar, 39 n. 6
Culture,
    Christian, 18
    crisis of, 82ff., 87

Davenson, Henri, 82, 86
De Ecclesia, 118 n. 1
Denzinger, 15 n. 1, 28 n. 1, 47 n. 7
Divino Afflante Spiritu, 16, 37, 84,
    95, 113 n. 3
Docetism, 31
    "biblical," 31
Doubts against faith, 22
Duguet, 13

Economy of revelation, 44
    God in, 22
Exegesis, 38, 113 n. 3
    literal, 98, 101ff.
    spiritual, 98, 101

Faith, 23, 27, 136ff.
Fathers of the Church, 25, 44, 47,
    69, 91, 94, 98, 118 n. 1
Focillon, Henri, 129
de Foucauld, Charles, 51, 73, 92 n.
    3
Francis of Assisi, St., 19, 73
Freedom, 84, 88

Gardeil, 84
Guardini, Romano, 93 n. 4

Hegelianism, Marxist, 89

Imagination, 116ff.
    as power of truth, 126ff.
Incarnation, the, 28f.
Inspiration, 30, 32, 34 n. 5
Intervention of God in human his-
    tory, 55ff., 85
Irenaeus, St., 47
Israel,
    expectation of, 58, 60
    People of God, 58
    "people of the promise," 59

Jesus Christ, mystery of, 63ff., 138
Jerome, St., 96
"Johannine problem," the, 22

Kenosis, 30
Kierkegaard, Søren, 87ff.
Koran, the, 32

Lacordaire, J. B., 133
Lagrange, 84
Langlois, 127
Language,
    biblical, 37
    human, 37f.
Leo XIII, Pope, 32 n. 3, 84
Literary genre, 34ff., 39, 117
Liturgical movement, 92f.
Liturgy, 93f., 98
Loisy, A. F., 83

Magisterium, 15f., 27, 47
Marrou, H. I., 128 n. 4

Metanoia, 130
Metaphysics, 87
Methodology, 84
Missionary movement, 92
Modernist, 83 n. 1, 85
Moslems, 32

New Testament, 62f., 67, 95, 98

Objectivity, historical, 86f.
Old Testament, 62ff., 67, 95, 97ff., 106
 content of, 104

Pascal, Blaise, 35, 63
Péguy, Charles, 39, 42, 109
Pius XII, Pope, 16, 37f., 84
Prayer, 76ff., 113ff.
Providentissimus Deus, 32 n. 3, 39, 84

Quesnel, P., 15

Reason, 84
Renan, J. E., 82, 85, 86
Revelation, 29, 34 n. 5, 105f.
Rosary, the, 78
Rostand, Jean, 93

Sacred history, 41, 45, 55ff., 59f., 90, 94, 104

economy of, 39, 56f.
 structure of, 41ff.
Salvation, 65
Seignobos, Charles, 127
Synave, P., 32 n. 4
"Synoptic problem," the, 21

Teresa of Avila, St., 109 n. 1
Theology, beginning of, 23
Thérèse of Lisieux, St., 51, 92 n. 3
Thomas Aquinas, St., 23, 32 n. 4
Transcendence,
 of freedom, 88
 of God, 23
 of the Word of God, 19
Truth, 36f., 39, 112, 116

Vatican I, 28, 47 n. 7, 68, 118 n. 1
Vernacular, 113
Verne, Jules, 24

Wahl, Jean, 87
Witnesses, biblical, 23
Word of God, the, 17f., 21, 38, 45, 68, 97
 is inexhaustible, 25
 mystery of, 13
 source of revelation, 15
 in tradition, 46